CORPORATE AND FOUNDATION SUPPORT

STRATEGIES FOR FUNDING EDUCATION IN THE 21ST CENTURY

Edited by Mary Kay Murphy

CASE Books

ISBN 0-89964-353-1
Printed in the United States of America

The Council for Advancement and Support of Education is the largest international association of educational institutions, with more than 2,900 colleges, universities, independent elementary and secondary schools in the United States, Canada, Mexico, the United Kingdom, and 29 other countries as members. Since 1974, CASE has helped its members build relationships with their communities, raise funds, market their institutions to prospective students, diversify the profession, and foster public support of education. CASE also offers various advancement resources, provides standards and an ethical framework for the profession, and works with other organizations to respond to public issues, while promoting education worldwide.

Visit CASE Books online at *www.case.org/books*

Book design: Fletcher Design
Editors: Shannon Joyce and Ellen Ryan
Staff Adviser: Patricia Jackson

CASE Books

Council for Advancement and Support of Education
1307 New York Avenue, NW
Suite 1000
Washington, DC 20005-4701

Contents

Foreword

Support from corporations and foundations represents an increasingly important component of an overall fund-raising program at many colleges and universities, especially those with a strong research mission or academic programs that relate closely to business interests. As state support of education decreases and expectations for an educational experience increase, private support will take on new importance in the 21st century, especially in the area of K–12 programs. Although the success of a corporate and foundation program at any given time will depend largely on the economy, increasingly, it will also depend on the management and sophistication of the program.

Since the first examples of corporate gifts in the 1920's, corporate giving has taken on a growing and evolving role in educational fund raising, reaching record highs in the 1980's. In the 1990's, corporate gifts began to change from unrestricted gifts to targeted gifts for defined purposes, purposes that fit into the companies' overall strategic plan. In this competitive and quid-pro-quo environment, educational institutions must plan and strategize in seeking corporate support. Institutions must thoroughly research a company and show it what benefit it will receive from relationships with educational institutions. They must plan how to solicit the gift and cultivate the relationship. Institutions must prove to a company that they have a sound budget and will manage the gift well. Finally, they must have a consistent and thorough recognition policy.

Likewise, foundation fund raising is an increasingly important component of a total educational fund-raising program, and one that will require much planning and strategy. Although foundation assets today total about $300 billion, there is growing competition for that money; higher education institutions must compete not only among each other but also with K-12 education, health agencies, and social welfare organizations. Just as in corporate fund raising, institutions must find out about a foundation's areas of interest and determine whether those interests actually match their institutions' strengths and needs. Colleges and universities must think long term in carrying out the long and complex process of grant proposals.

CASE has published this book to help educational institutions strategically make the most of the opportunities—and to handle the challenges—that corporate and foundation fund raising presents. Because corporate and foundation fund-raising programs are often combined at educational institutions, and because carrying out both kinds of fund raising takes many of the same skills and levels of planning, this book focuses on both corporate and foundation fund-raising. In the first section, six authors target issues common to both: ethics, legal issues, technology, program development, board involvement, and proposal writing. In the second section, five authors give ideas and tips for enhancing a corporate fund-raising program in the areas of internal institutional collaboration, branding opportunities, international corporations, fund raising at large research universities, and corporate support for K-12 education. In the final section, five authors discuss issues specific to foundation fund raising: strategic planning, internal collaboration, program development, funding consortia, and career development.

Through the wise and experienced counsel of Mary Kay Murphy, the book's editor, and the book's chapter authors, readers will gain an overview of corporate and foundation fund raising as well as learn innovative steps to building an effective program that works for their campuses.

Eustace Theodore
President, CASE
Washington, DC
March 2000

Preface

In 1989, the Council for Advancement and Support of Education published a book that I edited, *Cultivating Foundation Support for Education.* The book met a special need for those of us who were interested in raising private money from foundations to support education programs, projects, and priorities.

Although much remains constant in the area of foundation fund raising, many things have changed, including the amount of money available, the number of organizations (both in the U.S. and internationally) that are competing for the grants, the way foundations evaluate proposals, and what kinds of projects foundations will fund. The constants include the necessary role of prospect research, trustee and staff contacts with foundation leaders and program officers, and the importance of stewarding gifts to ensure they are used for their intended purpose. At the same time that foundation fund raising is evolving, corporate fund raising is also changing. All around you, you will see corporations partnering with education in altogether new ways and to new extents.

Of the total philanthropic funds made available to education, more support comes from individuals than from corporations or foundations. However, as we enter the 21st century, support from corporations and foundations is, and will remain, a lynchpin in the overall funding support for educational programs. The support ranges from buildings and renovations to scholarships and endowed chairs. In some instances, one source will fund the budget for an entire program (e.g. a Coca-Cola Scholars program); more commonly, multiple corporate or foundation sources will be needed to fund one program. Frequently, institutional funds must be invested in the project or program before corporate or foundation sources will make their investment.

Corporate and foundation fund raising is a vital component of development that must be strategically incorporated into a total institutional advancement plan. Toward that end, CASE has commissioned a new book that combines both corporate and foundation fund-raising strategies to support education in the new millennium.

I have been privileged to serve as the editor of this new book, the first that CASE published in 2000. Working with me to bring this book into production were 15 first-rate corporate and foundation officers. Their topics include, among others:

- How can you use technology to effectively enhance your corporate and foundation relations?
- How can you effectively coordinate board members' correspondence with funding sources?
- Should you segment your foundation program?
- What are the benefits of working in a funding consortium?
- How can you measure you program's productivity?
- How can you forge corporate partnerships that suit your institution's academic priorities?
- How can you integrate branding opportunities into your events?
- How can you ensure the necessary internal collaboration at your institution to have a successful program?
- How can your institution benefit from international corporate and foundation funding sources and how do you get such a program started?

These authors were recruited from some of the nation's leading private, public, four-year, research, and K-12 educational institutions. Their work has been innovative, cutting-edge, and significant. They bring their insight and experience to bear in sharing their proven successes with you. I am deeply thankful for their contributions.

I would also like to thank several key staff leaders at CASE. President Eustace Theodore, who wrote the foreword to this book, has been a source of stimulation and inspiration to me and to other leading practitioners in the institutional advancement profession in his tenure as CASE trustee, secretary of the board, and president. Vice President for Education Trish Jackson provided leads on authors and identified outstanding practitioners in the field for participation in this book. The CASE Books staff worked tirelessly and enthusiastically to bring this book to publication. Especially notable were Nancy Raley and Shannon Joyce.

I would like to dedicate this book to President Dolores E. Cross and the institutional advancement staff at Morris Brown College, where I am currently vice president for institutional advancement, for their dedication to corporate and foundation fund-raising fundamentals, their passion for improving educational opportunities for our college's faculty and students, and their commitment to using these fundamentals to move the college forward in the 21st century.

I would also like to dedicate this book to the graduate students that I teach in the Peabody College at Vanderbilt University master's degree sequence in institutional advancement. These outstanding professionals are dedicated and disciplined as they seek to expand the knowledge and refine the research that undergirds the institutional advancement profession we have come to know since the 1958 Greenbriar I Conference and its 1983 successor, the Greenbriar II Conference.

Mary Kay Murphy, Editor
Atlanta, Georgia
March 2000

SECTION I

Corporate and Foundation Support for the 21st Century

Ethics in Corporate and Foundation Fund Raising

Geoff Liggett
Former Director of Corporate and Foundation Relations
Carnegie Mellon University

1

The purpose of this chapter is to familiarize corporate and foundation officers with the ethical framework in which we operate as fund raisers and representatives of higher education in the nonprofit sector. This chapter will show you ways to explore your understanding of ethics, describe logical steps to ethical decision-making, and identify ethical challenges in modern corporate and foundation fund raising.

Defining Ethics

LORD MOULTON, A BRITISH LAWMAKER IN THE 19TH CENTURY, once said that "Ethics is obedience to the unenforceable, which should be contrasted with obedience to the enforceable—that's what law is."

Ethics and laws are both grounded in universal truths that almost all societies agree upon. However, unlike laws, ethics—obedience to the unenforceable—is hard to define. There is no fund raiser's counterpart to the NCAA, which routinely checks up on lapses in ethics and the breaking of rules. Likewise, most corporations have neither clearly defined rules of ethical conduct nor a system of sanctions. And while foundations with professional staffs and independent boards generally do have policies and procedures that clarify use of gifts and reporting standards, family or closely held foundations often do not make such policies explicit.

For most of us, ethical dilemmas in our work are less often a clear-cut right versus wrong and more often a matter of competing "rights." A corporate and foundation relations officer at a university travels among a number of different sectors (education, religion, business, government, and nonprofit) and, to be effective, needs to understand, interpret, and respond to many different ethical norms and expectations.

Understanding Ethics and Acting Ethically

ANY DISCUSSION OF ETHICS IN FUND RAISING, especially for those in education, begins with the fundamental understanding that ethical and moral behavior will result in trust between parties. The degree to which you succeed in cultivating and soliciting gifts for your institutions depends largely on the trust, integrity, credibility, and respect that you develop with the corporate and foundation leaders with whom you now interact. Your success also depends on the relationships and trust your predecessors built; after all, a typical foundation gives 25 percent of new foundation its new gifts to organizations they have given to previously.

Most of you serving in education believe in your institution's overall mission to better society by educating the next generation of leaders; expanding the realms of knowledge through research; and serving your local, national, and international communities. It is your responsibility to understand and maintain the highest standards of ethical conduct as you help your institutions raise funds from corporations and foundation to carry out this mission.

It is important to have an understanding of your personal and institutional ethics before facing a dilemma. If you are a manager, you have a responsibility to discuss ethics with your staff and to incorporate ethical decision-making into the everyday operation of your office. Organizations like CASE can provide case studies from which you can generate discussions in your own office. See a sample case study in ethics on page 5. Case studies are especially effective when discussed in a group setting, such as in ethics-related sessions at professional conferences or in-house with your institutional advancement staff.

As you continue to explore issues of ethics, review your institution's code of ethics and the professional codes with your supervisor or staff. You will find several names of professional organizations at the end of this chapter that have statements of ethics. CASE's statement of ethics appears on page 6 and NSFRE's "Standards of Professional Practice" appears on page 10 and "A Donor Bill of Rights" appears at the end of this chapter. An understanding of related legal issues is also helpful. See Chapter 2 for a brief discussion of legal issues in corporate and foundation relations.

In your discussions of ethics, consider the following factors:

- the law (local, state, and federal),
- your personal sense of what is right,
- your supervisor's opinion,

Excerpt of a Sample Case Study

(provided by CASE's National Clearinghouse for Ethics in Educational Fund Raising)

Ed Higgins, the new director of development for Southwest Technological University, has been reviewing file reports on STU's corporate donors. He learns that Plateau Gas and Electric Co. has consistently contributed substantial sums to support the Institute's School of Engineering. Harold Ender, who runs Plateau's Energy Resource Division, serves on the School's Visiting Committee and has been a personal contributor as well.

Ed pulls the file on Plateau and runs across a letter to Ender from Samuel McGill, dean of the school, acknowledging Plateau's most recent contribution and assuring him the "usual letter of agreement" from the development office will be forthcoming soon. He finds no "letter of agreement" in the file. When he encounters the dean, Ed asks about the letter.

"Oh, that's the same letter we send to Mid-State Power and High Mountain Hydro. You know, they're utility companies… It lets them classify what they give us as a 'cost of doing business' instead of as a contribution. That way, they can count it in their rate base… If what they give us is labeled a contribution, it takes a little nip out of net earnings. What they give us or anyone else is peanuts to them. If instead of counting it against earnings they can stick it in their rate-base, it doesn't amount to a hill of beans there either. But they'd rather do it that way, and it's OK with us."

"Still," Ed replies, "if I get what you're saying, Plateau's customers end up paying for the contributions instead of its stockholders."

"Yeah, but nobody notices. Nobody cares."

Later, Ed mentions the arrangement to Eve Wilson, the development office's corporate relations coordinator.

"Yeah, I know all about it and I think it stinks," Eve tells him. "I'm speaking as a Plateau customer, mind you, not as an officer of STU. Plateau's gotten themselves three rate increases out of the Public Utility Commission in five years. And I resent the idea they give money to the university and then turn around and use it to gouge little guys like me. So there—and if you tell anyone around here what I just said, I'll deny it!"

Two weeks later, Dean McGill tells Ed he thinks he can solicit Harold Ender for a leadership gift, perhaps even enough to put the chair in his name. That sounds promising, Ed tells the dean.

"By the way," Ed adds, "I've been thinking about these letters we write the utility companies. I know it doesn't amount to anything moneywise, but the idea of letting them put their gifts into their rate base bothers me. What if we didn't do it."

"If we stopped writing those letters," Dean McGill replies, "we'd stop getting those contributions. I know for damn sure that I'd have to start looking for someone else to fund this chair we're talking about. I'd just forget that idea, if I were you."

Ed thinks things over afterward. He acknowledges that how the corporations want to count their gifts really doesn't matter one way or the other in dollar terms. Neither stockholders nor customers are really helped or hurt. But the utility companies' support for the engineering school does matter quite a bit. And a leadership gift for the professorship would matter a lot.

Still, Ed is troubled by what he considers to be an ethical issue here – and he wants to resolve it.

DISCUSSION:

1. What parties have a legitimate stake in this issue? What are their respective rights and claims?
2. While the letters of agreement may be in STU's best financial interest, are there other considerations? What ethical principles underlie such considerations?
3. What are the implications for STU's institutional integrity of continuing the practice of sending letters of agreement to the utility companies? What is institutional integrity?
4. Though the letters don't seem to lead to any real financial burden on consumers, are there other considerations?
5. How persuasive is it that the engineering school stands to gain a major gift from Harold Ender? How do you weigh the school's potential gain with the potential consequences should the "letters of agreement" be discovered?
6. Is STU colluding in deception in this case?
7. What should Ed Higgins decide?

- the institution's ethical code (which may vary depending on whether you work for a religious, public, or private institution),
- your profession's guidelines (CASE, National Society for Fund Raising Executives, etc.), and

- ethical guidelines espoused by higher education and the nonprofit sector generally (e.g. NEA, Independent Sector, United Way).

Understanding Organizational Cultures

Organizational cultures influence how people make decisions and set expectations. You must be aware of both your organization's own culture and the ethical culture of the sectors in which you interact.

For example, a colleague who worked for many years in a small, private college had a difficult adjustment when she moved to a large public university's supporting foundation. The use of gifts (tickets to events, preferred parking, favorable treatment in admissions decisions) to cultivate and steward corporate donors at the larger institution would have been considered inappropriate at the smaller one where she previously worked. (Incidentally, some of these gift transactions have been curbed by recent changes in IRS rules, and more stringent and clear directives have been issued governing gifts and services offered in return for donations.)

> **CASE Statement of Ethics**
>
> Institutional advancement professionals, by virtue of their responsibilities within the academic community, represent their colleges, universities, and schools to the larger society. They have, therefore, a special duty to exemplify the best qualities of their institutions and to observe the highest standards of personal and professional conduct.
>
> In so doing, they promote the merits of their institutions, and of education generally, without disparaging other colleges and schools.
>
> Their words and actions embody respect for truth, fairness, free inquiry, and the opinions of others.
>
> They respect all individuals without regard to race, color, sex, sexual orientation, marital status, creed, ethnic or national identity, handicap, or age.
>
> They uphold the professional reputation of other advancement officers and give credit for ideas, words, or images originated by others.
>
> They safeguard privacy rights and confidential information.
>
> They do not grant or accept favors for personal gain, nor do they solicit or accept favors for their institutions where a higher public interest would be violated.
>
> They avoid actual or apparent conflicts of interest and, if in doubt, seek guidance from appropriate authorities.
>
> They follow the letter and spirit of laws and regulations affecting institutional advancement.
>
> They observe these standards and others that apply to their professions and actively encourage colleagues to join them in supporting the highest standards of conduct.
>
> *The CASE Board of Trustees adopted this Statement of Ethics to guide and reinforce our professional conduct in all areas of institutional advancement. The statement is also intended to stimulate awareness and discussion of ethical issues that may arise in our professional activities. The Board adopted the final text in Toronto on July 11, 1982, after a year of deliberation by national and district leaders and by countless volunteers throughout the membership.*

There are many other examples of situations in which knowing your institution's culture is essential. Corporate employers are becoming more aggressive in recruiting students. Some universities are now charging companies to come to campus to recruit students, a practice that would be considered unethical at other institutions. Find out where your institutional leadership stands on such issues before implementing new fund-raising programs.

Most foundation program officers operate under a strict code of ethics. For example, most never allow grantees or potential grantees to pay for the officer's meals. Or, if invited to campus to lecture or to be a part of a conference, most officers would never accept an honorarium or reimbursement for expenses. While these examples hold true for most foundations in the United States, it is not necessarily the same in other countries. For example, in some Asian cultures, gift giving (these gifts can take many different forms) is an expectation when VIPs (presidents, provosts, deans, trustees, corporate, foundation, and government leaders) meet. When traveling abroad or hosting foreign visitors, you as representatives of your institution should research the culture and expectations of the other country and also be able to explain your institution's culture. Doing so will help you avoid embarrassing ethical conflicts and ensure successful meetings and ethically sound exchanges.

Ethical Challenges

EVEN IF YOU HAVE COME TO AN UNDERSTANDING OF YOUR OWN ETHICS and the ethics of your institution, you will inevitably come across ethical challenges that will test your understanding.

One of the more important roles of corporate and foundation development officers is managing expectations for internal and external constituents. In soliciting and using a gift, you must consider the needs and priorities of both the institution and the corporate or foundation donor. This includes determining what benefits both the institution and the donor will receive from a relationship; stating what rights the donor and the institution will retain; and clarifying what level of control the institution and the donor will maintain in that relationship. Being prepared, knowing both the culture of your institution and the funding organization, thinking strategically, and being upfront in each of these exchanges will help you avoid ethical conflicts. Here are a few trends in modern campus fund raising that highlight potential areas of ethical conflicts.

Use of Gifts

One ethical pitfall in educational fund raising is the practice of "mirroring." This results when a fund raiser, faculty member, administrator, or student writes a proposal to mirror the interests of the potential donor either a) without carefully considering whether the funder and the grant recipients are a good match, or b) knowing that the institution will probably not be able to carry out the terms of the proposal. If it is indeed not a good match, the institution will have received the grant, but neither the institution's nor the funder's priorities will be met.

To avoid this trap, be clear about the institution's priorities and about how they align with the donor's interests. It is important that the institution's—and not your own—priorities lead the request. If you find a donor interested in funding scholarships for underrepresented minorities, yet the institution's infrastructure or commitment to recruiting minorities is not in place, you will quickly find yourself and your institution in a compromising situation: either unsuccessfully shading the truth to persuade the funder or losing credibility as you struggle to meet the restrictions of the gift.

There will always be a certain level of tension between opportunistic and strategic fund raising. This is healthy: Campuses need to respond to external influences to remain vital. However, the gifts you seek (cash for a specific purpose, products, real estate, and so on) must be useful to the institution. For instance, you should rarely solicit a gift with the intention of selling it. Reselling the gift within two years could create tax problems for the original donor. Likewise, your institution needs to use gifts of software or computer equipment as outlined in the acceptance agreement. Failure to do so risks unethical stewardship of solicited gifts and diminishes the chances of winning more gifts.

Three Crucial Moments

James Donohue, writing in the 1989 CASE Book *Cultivating Foundation Support for Education,* defines what he believes to be the essential values built into the very structure of foundation fund raising. They are: competition; trust; fairness and equality; and honesty and integrity.

He noted that in the relationship between a foundation and a university, there are three crucial moments where these ethical values come into play:

1) When foundations are determining what organization to fund,

2) When institutions are applying for funding, and

3) When the institution is using—and reporting on—the gift it has received. Below he spells out these three moments in this chapter excerpt.

> ....These [ethical] values come into play at three distinct moments [in the relationship between an institution and a foundation], which are, in fact, decision points where adhering to clear ethical standards is important: the point when the foundation identifies areas for grants; the application process; and the time after a grant award.
>
> **Identifying Areas for Funding**
>
> .... The decisions that foundations make about funding priorities are basically moral decisions, based on an understanding of the responsibility that goes with the role that foundations play in the larger scheme of society. Foundations exercise this responsibility when they make decisions about granting categories. It becomes attendant on them, therefore, to assess their choices in light of their effects on the long- and short-term future of society. This can be done by defining granting areas in accord with societal needs, as well as in accord with societal want and preference. In other words, the well-being of the human community is an important criterion that foundations must keep in mind when they decide what to grant as well as to whom to grant. . . Foundations need to find ways to assure those who make granting decisions will be aware of these types of considerations. The larger social welfare and health are at stake in these decisions.
>
> **The Application Process**
>
> .... Most institutions would hesitate to include false statements in a grant application; this is clearly wrong, and foundations have ways of verifying the accuracy of information provided in a proposal, so an institution would have little to gain and much to lose by going this route. But exaggeration is not such a simple issue. Since institutions, like many individuals, often have an inflated view of themselves, they tend to state their case in glowing terms, perhaps exaggerating the success of an earlier project. When the result is to describe an institution (or a project) as something it is not, the application may be creating a relationship based on skewed perceptions that can lead to situations where expectations and actions clash. In this light, then, it is difficult to condone exaggeration in foundation fund raising. A relationship based on honesty and reality will be stronger and more successful over the long term.
>
> How, then, can an institution that has chosen complete honesty compete successfully if other applicants are exaggerating their claims? This is where trust is essential. When the grant seeker believes the foundation is capable of piercing through the exaggerations of competing institutions to judge a case on the merits, the application process works well....
>
> Candor, then, is the responsibility of both parties: The applying institutions must be honest, and the foundation staff must be able to discount those who are not honest.
>
> **After the Grant Has Been Received**
>
> .... Numerous opportunities [for ethical wrongdoings] do not end with the award of the grant. On the contrary, numerous opportunities arise in the use of the grant money and the reporting of this use. To use a grant for a different purpose than that stipulated in the award is clearly wrong. Such a misuse compromises the whole system of foundation fund raising.
>
> But a more troubling issue is the way foundation grants are reported and categorized in the financial records of the receiving institution. In efforts to reach stated goals or to project to the public a successful track record, institutions may take liberties with the way gifts are reported and classified. For example, the fiscal years to which grants are applied are sometimes blurred, the status of the award altered to qualify for matching funds or to meet an announced campaign goal.
>
> .... Deceptive practices run the obvious risk of being discovered by the auditors or the public. An equally serious problem, however, is the effect this kind of behavior has on the institution's long-range character, both in the eyes of its internal constituency and in the eyes of the public. It inevitably weakens the institution's stature over the long term.
>
> ....We need to develop ways in which the profession, the foundations, and the institutions themselves can monitor behavior and enforce sanctions when infractions have been committed.

Be familiar with your institution's gift-acceptance policies. This will help to prevent you from over-promising a donor about arrangements with your institution.

A trend in giving, especially among corporations, is that relationships with campuses are increasingly based on an exchange of services, instead of a gift. It is important for the institution's representative in these negotiations to ensure that gifts are used appropriately. Corporate gifts should always include a document outlining the purpose and value of the gift, including clearly defined and verified restrictions by the donor. This, the first step in stewardship of the gift or grant, will be an important reference tool for future correspondence with the donor. Given the relatively frequent changes in personnel in both business and academe, accurate and complete gift records are essential.

The corporate trend toward giving gifts to institutions as part of a cause-related marketing strategy is another ethical concern. The motivation behind such corporate "gifts" is not to better society but to promote a company's image or product. Be clear about what each organization expects to gain from these transactions/relationships.

> There will always be a certain level of tension between opportunistic and strategic fund raising.

If your institution decides to change the use of a gift, inform the donor as soon as possible. Although this sounds simple, when gifts must be returned, it is most often because of a lack of communication with the donor when problems arise on campus about the use of the gift. Again, trust, integrity (yours and the institution's), and the future of the donor relationship are at stake. Even if a portion of a gift needs to be returned, your honorable actions will put you and your institution in a position to continue your philanthropic relationship with the donor.

Vendor Benefits

Soliciting vendors for gifts, products, and services can present other ethical dilemmas. Issues including the timing of bidding on contracts, alumni-owned businesses, and the benefits of a gift versus discounting of the product or service all need to be carefully examined.

To avoid conflicts, many successful development offices have developed a close working relationship with the business office. Ideally, this relationship would begin with a discussion of the development officer's goals and objectives; the chief financial officer or purchasing offer would then carefully assess the pros and cons of soliciting a particular vendor. The director of purchasing would ensure that all potential vendors have the same opportunity to compete/participate in the bidding process and that any gifts from the vendor would not be offset by higher prices of the product or service to the school. As business and philanthropic agendas are being joined, a way to start this process is to select a small but significant subset of vendors and deal with them on a case by case basis until proper communication channels and trust are established.

Recruiting Privileges

The practice of soliciting funds from organizations that also recruit your students poses other potential conflicts. Ethical purists would argue that companies that donate to an institution should not be treated preferentially when recruiting students. This is an especially difficult area to con-

NSFRE Standards of Professional Practice

Adopted and incorporated into the NSFRE Code of Ethical Principles, November 1992

Furthermore, while striving to act according to the above values, NSFRE members agree to abide by the NSFRE Standards of Professional Practice, which are adopted and incorporated into the NSFRE Code of Ethical Principles. Violation of the Standards may subject the member to disciplinary sanctions, including expulsion, as provided in the NSFRE Ethics Enforcement Procedures.

Professional Obligations

1. Members shall not engage in activities that harm the member's organization, clients, or profession.
2. Members shall not engage in activities that conflict with their fiduciary, ethical, and legal obligations to their organizations and their clients.
3. Members shall effectively disclose all potential and actual conflicts of interest; such disclosure does not preclude or imply ethical impropriety.
4. Members shall not exploit any relationship with a donor, prospect, volunteer or employee to the benefit of the member or the member's organization.
5. Members shall comply with all applicable local, state, provincial, federal, civil and criminal laws.
6. Members recognize their individual boundaries of competence and are forthcoming and truthful about their professional experience and qualifications.

Solicitation and Use of Charitable Funds

7. Members shall take care to ensure that all solicitation materials are accurate and correctly reflect the organization's mission and use of solicited funds.
8. Members shall take care to ensure that donors receive informed, accurate and ethical advice about the value and tax implications of potential gifts.
9. Members shall take care to ensure that contributions are used in accordance with donors' intentions.
10. Members shall take care to ensure proper stewardship of charitable contributions, including timely reports on the use and management of funds.
11. Members shall obtain explicit consent by the donor before altering the conditions of a gift.

Presentation of Information

12. Members shall not disclose privileged or confidential information to unauthorized parties.
13. Members shall adhere to the principle that all donor and prospect information created by, or on behalf of, an organization is the property of that organization and shall not be transferred or utilized except on behalf of that organization.
14. Members shall give donors the opportunity to have their names removed from lists that are sold to, rented to, or exchanged with other organizations.
15. Members shall, when stating fund-raising results, use accurate and consistent accounting methods that conform to the appropriate guidelines adopted by the American Institute of Certified Public Accountants (AICPA)* for the type of organization involved. (* In countries outside of the United States, comparable authority should be utilized.)

Compensation

16. Members shall not accept compensation that is based on a percentage of charitable contributions; nor shall they accept finder's fees.
17. Members may accept performance-based compensation, such as bonuses, provided such bonuses are in accord with prevailing practices within the members' own organizations, and are not based on a percentage of charitable contributions.
18. Members shall not pay finder's fees, commissions or percentage compensation based on charitable contributions and shall take care to discourage their organizations from making such payments.

Reprinted with permission from NSFRE. Complete code of ethical principles appears on *www.nsfre.org.*

trol as administrative and academic departments, increasingly pressured to generate income from these corporations, may use this as a perk in the corporations' relationship with the campus. A guiding principle here might be to avoid perks to companies that smack of "exclusiveness." Giving preference to one company is one thing; excluding other companies from doing something entirely is another.

Confidentiality Rights

As you search for the best practices, you will increasingly encounter corporations and institutions that desire the ability to benchmark. Many corporations want to know how best to position themselves by finding out the amount and purpose of their competition's gifts to a group of target schools. However, many corporations and foundations do not publicize details of their grantmaking, and most corporations would rather not publicize the extent of their relationship with any particular institution.

To respond to requests for this information, you might put together some general information, grouping contributors according to the range of their donations. Otherwise, obtain donors' permission before releasing specific information about their gifts. Rules on this may differ depending on whether you work for a public or a private institution.

Be aware that research documents, e-mail, and other reports and correspondence can be subpoenaed. Be sure that sensitive information is communicated only to those who need to know and generally not committed to paper or computer files.

Control and Accountability

Often along with a donation, a company or foundation will demand a high level of accountability and a certain amount of control over the use of the gift. How you will report to your donors, and what input they will have in the use of the gift, should be determined and shared with key administrators ahead of time.

Personal foundations are increasingly important players in philanthropy. These are usually family foundations without professional staff, annual reports, or Web sites. Many are created by entrepreneurs who demand a high level of accountability in their businesses but are not well informed about the differences between business and ethical considerations when it comes to the logistics of philanthropic giving.

These donors also often expect to have a measure of control, which presents a greater possibility that they will use the institution to further a political or personal agenda. The donor may ask to be involved in organizational decisions such as who receives scholarships and professorships, what architects will be chosen for the design of new buildings, and how their gift will be managed. All of the above are the purview of the faculty and administration—they are academic and management decisions that must be carefully considered. The fund raiser and key administrators must be fully informed about the donor and the proposed gift and not make premature promises to the donor that cannot be fulfilled.

The changing nature of corporate and foundation relationship building requires the close interaction of the business, purchasing, contract research, general counsel, technology transfer, research, student affairs, and public relations offices on campus. Knowing where a project and its potential funding start and stop and who should handle the stages of the project are increasingly complex tasks.

Foundations, for example, are making larger commitments in the form of program-related investments (PRI) to complement their grantmaking. A PRI is a business loan in furtherance of the foundation's philanthropic objectives; it is not a gift. With PRI's, the foundation is generally entitled to much more control over the terms of its investment than it would have over a gift. Fund raisers need to adjust their own understanding and expectations, and the institution's, for these new forms of capital. These more complicated gift transactions require that the development office develop solid working relationships with the business offices on their campuses.

Campuses are also under increasing pressure to be more accountable and to adopt the business practices of the private sector. Since the mid-1990's, there has been much attention paid to the means by which fund raisers are being compensated—for example, incentive-based pay, performance-based pay, and bonuses. This issue will be interesting to monitor because it encompasses what motivates people in nonprofit fund raising, the purposes of philanthropy, and the mission of higher education.

Conclusion

THE GOAL OF THIS CHAPTER IS TO GIVE YOU AS CORPORATE AND FOUNDATION officers ways to work toward an understanding of your own ethics and the ethical cultures of the institutions where you work and the corporations and foundations with which you interact and examples of inherent tensions in today's marketplace. Integrity is everything in the development business. Preserving it requires constant and consistent attention.

REFERENCES AND ADDITIONAL RESOURCES

Direct Marketing Association. *Ethical Guidelines for Direct Marketers.* New York: Direct Marketing Association, 1999. (See also *www.the-dma.org*)

Koziol, Kenneth G. (ed.) and the Institute for Nonprofit Organization Management. *Ethics in Nonprofit Management: A Collection of Cases.* 2nd ed. San Francisco, CA: University of San Francisco, 1998
Contains teaching cases that instructors and workshop leaders can use in the study of ethics in nonprofit organization management. Each case presents a dilemma designed to stimulate moral reasoning; discussion questions are included for each case.

National Charities Information Bureau. *Standards in Philanthropy.* New York: National Charities Information Bureau, 1992. *(www.give.org/standard.cfm)*

National Committee on Planned Giving. *Model Standards for the Charitable Gift Planner.* Indianapolis: National Committee on Planned Giving, 1999. *(www.ncpg.org)*

National Society of Fund Raising Executives. *Guidelines to the Standards of Professional Practice.* Alexandria, VA: NSFRE, 1995.
Guidelines for interpreting and using the Code of Ethical Principles and Standards of Professional Practice. Includes examples.

National Society of Fund Raising Executives. *Code of Ethical Principles and Standards of Professional Practice* Alexandria, VA: NSFRE, 1991. *(www.nsfre.org)*

Philanthropic Advisory Service of the Better Business Bureau. *CBBB Standards for Charitable Solicitation.* Arlington, VA: Better Business Bureau, 1982. *(www.bbb.org)*

• • •

The following organizations publish professional statements of ethics:

- Association of Professional Researchers for Advancement (*www.apra.org*)
- Council for Advancement and Support of Education (*www.case.org*)
- Council on Foundations (*www.cof.org*)
- National Society of Fund Raising Executives (*www.nsfre.org*)
- National Association of Colleges and Employers (*www.jobweb.org/NACE/*)
- Institute for Global Ethics (*www.globalethics.org*)

A Donor Bill of Rights

Philanthropy is based on voluntary action for the common good. It is a tradition of giving and sharing that is primary to the quality of life. To assure that philanthropy merits the respect and trust of the general public, and that donors and prospective donors can have full confidence in the not-for-profit organizations and causes they are asked to support, we declare that all donors have these rights:

1. To be informed of the organization's mission, of the way the organization intends to use donated resources, and of its capacity to use donations effectively for their intended purposes.
2. To be informed of the identity of those serving on the organization's governing board, and to expect the board to exercise prudent judgment in its stewardship responsibilities.
3. To have access to the organization's most recent financial statements.
4. To be assured their gifts will be used for the purposes for which they were given.
5. To receive appropriate acknowledgment and recognition.
6. To be assured that information about their donations is handled with respect and with confidentiality to the extent provided by law.
7. To expect that all relationships with individuals representing organizations of interest to the donor will be professional in nature.
8. To be informed whether those seeking donations are volunteers, employees of the organization, or hired solicitors.
9. To have the opportunity for their names to be deleted from mailing lists that an organization may intend to share.
10. To feel free to ask questions when making a donation and to receive prompt, truthful, and forthright answers.

The text of this statement in its entirety was developed by the American Association of Fund-Raising Counsel (AAFRC), Association for Healthcare Philanthropy (AHP), Council for Advancement and Support of Education (CASE), and National Society of Fund Raising Executives (NSFRE).

Legal Issues and Corporate and Foundation Support

Kent M. Weeks
Attorney at Law
Weeks, Anderson, Russell, Haynes + Baler
Professor, the Practice of Education
Peabody College at Vanderbilt University

2

Nonprofit 501(c)(3) institutions are increasingly subject to scrutiny. The government and donor organizations, including corporations and foundations, are continually reviewing the performance of nonprofit institutions to ensure they operate legally and ethically.

Educational institutions need to review and apply accepted guidelines on gift reporting and evaluation. They must determine when the donor's proposed control and benefits nullify the requirements of a gift. To qualify as a gift, its payment must be a voluntary transfer of money or property made without receipt of, or expectation of, commensurate return benefit. In these areas, the institution must carefully analyze the proposed gift and its compliance with institutional policies, guidelines, and Internal Revenue Service rules.

Nonprofit Status

EDUCATIONAL INSTITUTIONS MUST DEMONSTRATE COMPLIANCE with the requirements for 501(c)(3) tax-exempt status. Corporations and foundations do not want to make major gifts to campuses whose alleged violation of their nonprofit status ensnares them in legal difficulties and adverse publicity.

Most corporations and foundations will require the recipient institution to document its nonprofit 501(c)(3) status. Given the current headlines about misuse of this status, these funders need to ensure that the entity they're funding is not under IRS scrutiny and that its tax-exempt status is not in jeopardy. Because nonprofits must provide anyone, on request, with their IRS Form 990 and other tax-exempt documents, though, this is not an onerous requirement.

Funders may also seek to ensure that the institution is complying with applicable charitable solicitation laws or is exempt from compliance with state regulatory systems.

For institutions, disclosure requirements, concern over the valuation of some gifts, and conflict-of-interest requirements governing top officers' compensation are making 501(c)(3) compliance an ever-growing challenge. And campuses must be careful not to step over the not-so-distinct line on excessive lobbying, thereby risking exposure to IRS review and excise taxes.

There is also the obligation to carry out the purposes of gifts. In a few cases, institutions may encounter difficulty at this and need to seek advice from the donor or apply for court approval to use the gift differently. In a widely monitored case, a foundation recently sued the University of Bridgeport over whether the foundation could enforce a gift's restrictions in spite of a subsequent change at the university in the circumstances surrounding the gift's purpose.

The university argued that only the state attorney general had the authority to enforce the terms of a completed gift. The Supreme Court of Connecticut ruled 3-to-2 that the foundation did not have standing to challenge subsequent use of the gift. This litigation highlights the fact that funders have a continuing interest in whether their gifts are used for their intended purposes.

Reporting Standards

BOTH CASE/NACUBO REPORTING STANDARDS and FASB 116-117 standards apply to the reporting and accounting of corporate and foundation gifts. These reporting standards will not normally raise major issues. In case of doubt about reporting obligations, consult auditors or internal accountants.

What is a Gift?

A GIFT IS A VOLUNTARY TRANSFER OF PROPERTY by a donor to a recipient without consideration. There are three essentials for a gift: intent, delivery, and acceptance. For a completed gift to be tax-deductible, two conditions must be met: The donor relinquishes control over the property and the donor does not directly benefit from the gift.

It usually is obvious when a donor relinquishes control. There are cases, however, when corporations and foundations attempt to control the gift. Such action triggers legitimate questions of whether a gift has been made. Even if control is not prohibitive, donor requirements may run counter to institutional gift policies.

If the donor directly benefits from the gift, it is not actually a gift. For example, if a donor makes a contribution to a church but the money is used to pay the donor's child's tuition, the contribution is not a gift and is not tax-deductible.

Four types of gifts prompt legal questions of definition and valuation: gifts with donor restrictions, matching gifts, gifts in kind, and quid pro quo gifts.

Gifts with Donor Restrictions

Corporations are often willing to make major gifts or grants such as endowed chairs. A corporation may seek to ensure that its endowment will support particular research. There is generally no problem with these mutual agreements. When the corporation insists on too much control in selecting faculty members or operating the program, however, questions arise over whether a gift has been made and whether the restrictions conflict with institutional gift policy. Gift policies may prohibit accepting gifts when the donor attempts to control the research grant or when there are significant requirements for program content.

In 1995, the United Parcel Service offered the University of Washington Medical School $2.5 million to establish a research chair in occupational orthopedics. The donation was contingent on granting both tenure and the chair to a particular researcher. The professor's research claimed that back injuries relate more to poor workout attitudes than to workplace ergonomics, an argument consistent with UPS's opposition to recent U.S. government efforts to impose ergonomic standards.

The university held to its position that the chair holder would be appointed by the dean after being selected by a search committee in accordance with university policies and procedures. Even though the parties appeared to be reaching agreement in March 1997, the UPS foundation declared it was in no position to endow the chair. The UPS Foundation based its withdrawal on the fact that it had stopped endowing chairs in the 1970s.

If the donor directly benefits from the gift, it is not actually a gift.

The case indicates the importance of determining how much control a donor will have and how that control might trigger legal issues and potential violations of institutional gift policy or academic freedom.

Matching Gifts

Many corporations also sponsor matching gift programs. These programs can benefit education immensely, but they can also be abused. A matching gift could be allocated to a specific program, such as athletics, not intended by the corporate matcher. Or the gift might somehow provide the individual donor a privilege or benefit that raises questions about whether a gift has been made.

The individual donor may benefit in ways the corporate sponsor did not contemplate—and, if the individual donor benefits, the gift may not be tax-deductible. These cases point to the need to clarify the corporation-campus relationship and the corporation's expectations. Institutions must consult the CASE/NACUBO guidelines on the treatment of matching gifts.

Gifts in Kind

Gifts in kind require adherence to valuation and reporting requirements. Corporations seek the maximum charitable deduction, and institutions want to facilitate that goal—while following the explicit rules for valuing gifts in kind.

When corporations donate personal property, usually the institution is obligated to assign the property a value for reporting purposes. The burden is on the corporation to determine the gift's value, although when the amount exceeds $5,000, an independent appraisal is required. The basis on which these gifts are valued may raise significant concerns if the institution is concerned about the appraisal or subsequently decides to sell the gift within a two-year period.

Quid Pro Quo Gifts

Corporations and foundations are strategic in their giving. Accordingly, they seek benefits from their gifts. Many corporations and foundations align themselves with campus cultural, social, educational, and athletic events to improve their image or communicate a specific message.

These gifts could be seen as intermingling with business deals. One university is now responding to allegations that it received foundation money to further its relationship with a business owned by the foundation's donor. Arrangements such as this raise important legal issues for the foundation, the business, and the university. Individual donors also receive services or goods as a result of a charitable gift.

There are very explicit tax rules for evaluating how much of the gift is charitable and how much is a return for service. The IRS continually reviews how certain gifts that benefit donors should be treated for tax purposes. Recently, after a major look at the tax treatment of corporate boxes for athletic events, the IRS affirmed its current rule that 80 percent of the lease payment is tax-deductible.

In a reverse situation, institutions may overreach and use their leverage to pry gifts, for example, from potential student applicants. Contributions-for-admissions schemes are unethical. When an institution bases admission on a gift, both fraud and a misuse of the charitable contribution have occurred. What is wrong is tying the making of a gift to admission. Consideration of the status of applicants, such as children of major donors, does not seem to violate this legal statute.

Affinity Marketing Programs

THE ATTORNEYS GENERAL OF 16 STATES recently challenged affinity marketing programs and the relationships between corporations and recipient organizations. The state officials are concerned that some promotional activities may mislead the public into thinking that recipients approve or endorse the corporate product or service. The attorneys general believe some of these marketing efforts could involve fraud or misleading advertising under state consumer-protection laws. Institutions need to clarify corporate relationships when product or service endorsements may be implied.

Conclusion

WITH THE NEW CORPORATE AND FOUNDATION PHILANTHROPIC EMPHASIS on strategic giving, new opportunities and challenges confront educational institutions. Careful assessment of gifts is necessary, clarity on the purpose of the gift is required, and compliance with ethical and legal standards is essential.

REFERENCES AND ADDITIONAL RESOURCES

Council for Advancement and Support of Education. *CASE Management Reporting Standards.* Washington, DC: CASE, 1996.

Council for Advancement and Support of Education (in cooperation with National Association of College and University Business Officers). *Guidelines for the Administration of Matching Gift Programs.* Washington, DC: CASE, 1990.

Council for Advancement and Support of Education (in cooperation with National Association of College and University Business Officers). *The Impact of FASB Standards 116 & 117 on Development Operations.* Washington, DC: CASE, 1995.

Herzog Foundation v. University of Bridgeport, 699 A.2d 995 (Conn. 1997).

Kraus, Ronald J., "The Changing Face of Corporate Giving," CURRENTS 25, no. 2 (February 1998): 10.

Rainbolt, William, "Gifts That Can't Be Matched," CURRENTS 13, no. 1 (January 1987): 12.

Taylor, John H., "Your Noncash Gift Questions Answered," CURRENTS 24, no. 7 (July/August 1998): 46.

Technology in Corporate and Foundation Support

Alan H. Bloomgarden
Assistant Director of Faculty Grants and Government Relations
Smith College

3

Computers and related technologies have revolutionized the workplace. This is as true in corporate and foundation grant seeking as it is anywhere else. Success in finding and managing corporate and foundation support for higher education now depends extensively on skillful use of computers to research and organize information about funders and funding opportunities and to communicate that information to colleagues and campus constituents. Figure 3-1 illustrates the range of technology resources now shaping corporate and foundation fund raising and relationships among them. If you're seeking corporate and foundation support, this figure shows your professional perspective on the "information superhighway."

Electronic Research and Communications: Finding Information and Staying Informed

MUCH OF THE INFORMATION ABOUT CORPORATE AND FOUNDATION GIVING that you once could glean only from thick, and sometimes dated, print directories is now available in a searchable, electronic form. The main advantages brought by this development include:

Fig 3-1. Range of Technological Resources

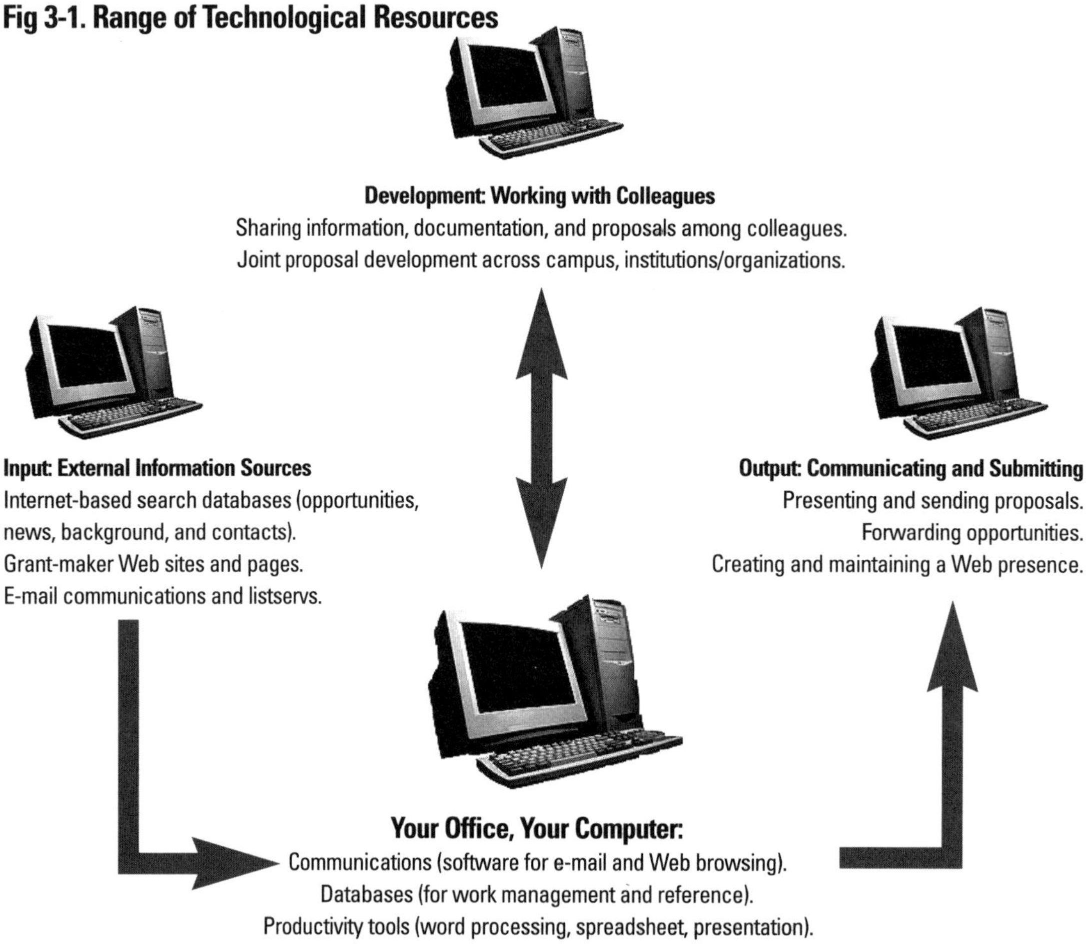

- speedy and focused access to the data you seek and
- improved opportunities for publishers to update their data more frequently than they could in print.

These improvements come at a price, but the features and timeliness of both online and CD-ROM/disk-based databases can make them well worth the investment. Table 3-1 lists some generalized funding databases, both online and CD-ROM- or disk-based databases that you can purchase. Many more specialized databases focusing on individual areas (e.g., arts, sciences, humanities) are also available in a searchable form both on the Internet and on disk/CD-ROM.

Table 3-1. Funding Databases

Internet-Based Funding Databases	***CD-ROM or Disk-based Databases***
Community of Science – *www.cos.com*	FCSearch (The Foundation Center)
IRIS – *www.iris.com*	KR OnDisc (Knight-Ridder)
SPIN – *www.spin.com*	
ORYX – *www.oryxpress.com/gs.htm*	

Exploring Grant-Maker Web Sites

Make the assumption that a Web site exists, because having one is increasingly a PR prerequisite. What can you expect to find? Contact information is the most basic resource, and this is sometimes provided with direct e-mail links to staff. Increasingly, funders' Web sites also offer program guidelines, application forms, annual reports or information on past giving, and links to grantees' Web sites. Requests for information are sometimes accepted through the site. The Foundation Center is perhaps the best place to begin researching charitable foundations and their giving. Visit the Foundation Center Web site at *www.fdncenter.org/onlib/ufg/index.html.*

Internet News and Directory Searches

Seek out other information about your prospective funding source even if it has a comprehensive and informative presence on its own Web site. Find out what others are saying potential funders are up to. Find out how and what grantees or "partners" are doing—credits for support often appear in research papers, advertising brochures, and conference programs posted by institutions engaging in work similar to that you seek to fund.

News sources are plentiful on the Internet. Retain a journalist's skepticism about the reliability of your sources, though, and remember that no one source or search tool is truly comprehensive; you must consult several. Still, Internet search engines can help you obtain valuable information about your target prospects and about the project areas you are seeking to fund. Alta Vista, Hotbot, Lycos, and Metacrawler are good search engines to start with.

Keeping Current

While many newspapers post some articles on their Web sites, fee-based news databases from information brokers such as Lexis-Nexis, Information Access, and Dialog provide more complete, timely, and highly searchable texts from a large number of major and regional newspapers, magazines, wire services, and other print sources.

Some companies provide news-clipping services that monitor topics or prospects for you, sending you customized collections of texts or data daily without your having to search. Of note also are the Federal Information Exchange (FEDIX) and other similar DC-based information providers, which are important sources of news and opportunities about federal funding and legislation. Which services you buy will depend on your budget, your work style and capabilities, and, more generally, your office's priorities.

Regardless, consider sharing your subscription with other offices on campus or in an institutional consortium. Internal partners can split the annual fees, and external partners can help negotiate group rates. For example, the Smith College office of corporate, foundation, and government relations shares its subscription fees for certain faculty grant-related sources with the office of the dean of the faculty. As an institutional member of the Five Colleges consortium, Smith also subscribes jointly with Amherst, Hampshire, Mount Holyoke, and the University of Massachusetts to purchase online resources at a lower consortial rate.

E-mail offers another vital means of staying on top of news and developments important to your pursuit of funds. Corporate and foundation officers network informally by creating lists of colleagues at similar institutions with whom they share questions or comments and swap information and updates on funding agencies, requests for proposals (RFPs), and grant awards. Some professionals share information through managed listservs, distribution lists that automatically send electronic mail messages posted by one participant to all list subscribers.

Listservs and Internet public newsgroups will frequently archive postings so they can be browsed or searched. Search engines like Alta Vista, Go.com, and Deja.com are just a few that can scan these resources on demand. For corporate and foundation relations work, the listserv CFRnet is a place to start: Send an e-mail message <subscribe cfrnet your name> to *listproc@medicine.wustl.edu.* Leave the subject line blank, and leave off any signature line you normally attach to your messages. See *http://philanthropy-review.com /forums* for a good starting point to find other lists of interest. Here are a few good lists to start with:

- ARNOVA-L for nonprofit organizations and voluntary action: *rlohman@wvnvm.wvnet.edu*
- PRSPCT-L prospect-research list: *listserv@uic.edu*
- GRANTS-L, fund raising, grants administration, and Internet resources: *listserv@gsuvml.gsu.edu*
- USNONPROFIT-L, a mailing list mirroring the soc.org.nonprofit newsgroup: *majordomo@rain.org*

Managing Project and Proposal Development

COMPUTER NETWORKS ARE INCREASINGLY VALUABLE AVENUES for sharing text and graphics or even video and sound that you can use in preparing project proposals and reports. Project managers and proposal developers commonly share files on internal networks and over the Web, and you can send formated documents, pictures, graphs, and data files as e-mail attachments to share and revise work in progress. Boilerplate information concerning your institution or project can be posted for access by multiple colleagues.

Besides the standard desktop tools of word processing, spreadsheet, and multimedia presentation software, corporate and foundation support seekers use database and integrated software packages to manage their contacts and schedules, to remind themselves of upcoming report or proposal deadlines, and to cross-reference grantmaker contacts (board members, program personnel) with prospect research, professional affiliations, and alumni databases on campus. The names and types of these packages are too numerous to list; however, the most basic advice is to choose packages that are compatible not only with your personal or office's work style and needs but also with each other. Sharing data and reports between systems is a common requirement for prospect tracking, stewardship, and proposal generation.

Getting Proposals Out and Managing a Web Presence

ALTHOUGH THE FABLED "PAPERLESS SOCIETY" MAY REMAIN still more dream than reality, some funding agencies are nonetheless moving toward completely electronic proposal submission. Leading the way are government agencies such as the National Science Foundation (and soon the National Institutes of Health); in the arena of private institutions, the Howard Hughes Medical Institute has developed an impressive Web-based proposal submission and reporting tool. More corporate and foundation grant makers are likely to introduce these soon.

Such tools bypass the print production stage for proposals and reports by either allowing applicants to prepare proposals using word processors, spreadsheets, and graphics software or requiring applicants to insert data, text, and graphics into forms over the Web. The latter scenario is more rigid and sometimes unnerving, as your proposal resides on your prospective funder's computer and you don't even get to see it put together until the end. But this is probably the route many grant makers will take because this format allows them to organize their processes and data better for their own purposes. In fact, a consortium led by the American Cancer Society is pushing this process further along; see its Web site at *www.gepps.org*.

Corporate and foundation grant seekers can prepare for the eventuality of online proposals by getting familiar with electronic submission facilities early in the testing phase, as they become available rather than when they have become required. Monitor the development of electronic submission tools, and organize your own data and text in electronic spreadsheets and word-processing files that are compatible.

Your institution's and your office's Web presence may be as significant to your prospects as their information was to you. They may visit your Web site to learn about your institution or project, and you should assume they will. You greatly enhance your ability to promote your efforts by ensuring that your institution maintains an updated, informative, and easily found Web site. Such a presence can permit you to supplement what you were able to squeeze within a page-limited proposal or promotional brochure.

You greatly enhance your ability to promote your efforts by ensuring that your institution maintains an updated, informative, and easily found Web site.

A Web site can also yield unsolicited interest in your project, as potential partners and supporters find you through the exploration of their own interests. A page containing information useful to students, scholars, and administrators, or one with connecting links to other pertinent resources, can be a valuable demonstration of your project's established place and competence within its field. Finally, your own office's Web site can be an efficient and timely means of communicating grant opportunities to students, faculty, and administrators: See, for example, the University of Florida's *F.Y.I.* newsletter at *www.ortge.ufl.edu/fyi.*

Trends

SEVERAL TRENDS THAT WILL SHAPE THE WAYS PROPOSALS are presented and handled at both ends of the process are worth highlighting. Multimedia presentations offer increasingly attractive possibilities for making your pitch. It is already technically possible to take a complex project idea, organizational maps, preliminary research, or evidence of a project's track record and create a Web site or a presentation package that includes graphics, video, and sound as well as text. The application of these technologies to proposal development may not be far off. Even after the gee-whiz factor wears thin, the possibilities for communicating sophisticated content may warrant judicious use of such facilities.

One development of special interest to corporate and foundation grant seekers is the Internal Revenue Service's effort to make the Form 990 required annually from all US 501(c)(3) charitable organizations available in a searchable database on the Web. The Form 990 can be an invaluable source of information about a prospective funder and its giving. See the Web site *www.form990.gov* for this work now under development. The Minnesota Council of Nonprofits has helped put that state's nonprofits' 990s on the Internet (see *www.mncn.org*); check with grantmaker or nonprofit councils in your state to track their progress.

The possibilities that such Web facilities create for public disclosure and responsiveness are immense. The Internet has literally created a revolution in the federal government's public relations work. Government agencies are in some cases leading the way toward making data, program announcements, guidelines, application materials, and financial management tools available.

Increasing electronic administration of corporate and foundation support seems a "virtual" certainty. Some funders may ask only that you submit funding requests and reports via e-mail or the Web; others will expect regular or constant updates with financial details, research and participant data, and project progress. As you increase your expectations that funders will present information to you via Web sites, so will their expectations rise about what information you will have available there.

REFERENCES AND ADDITIONAL RESOURCES

Bentz Whaley Flessner. *Resources for Prospect Development.* (www.bwf.com)

Brenann, T. *High-Tech Ties that Bind.* CURRENTS 25, No.9 (October 1999).

Facciponti, P.A. *Coping with Communication Overload: How to Stay Efficient and Sure in Today's Electronic World.* CURRENTS 22, No. 4 (April 1996).

Reindelback, D. *Web Worries: The World Wide Web Has Brought Possibilities and Problems. Here's How to Handle Troubling Topics of Access, Copyright, and Security.* CURRENTS 22, No. 10 (Nov/Dec 1996)

Watson, K. Electronic Expertise. CURRENTS 22, No. 7 (July/Aug 1996).

Program Development for Corporate and Foundation Support

Patricia J. Gregory
Senior Director of Corporate and Foundation Relations
Washington University School of Medicine in St. Louis

4

Seeking corporate and foundation support has become a specialty in great demand, thanks to the booming assets of foundations and the challenges of securing corporate support. Success requires close interaction with faculty, leaders, and other units of your institution as well as extensive knowledge about institutional strengths. Careful assessment of your institution's environment for corporate and foundation fund raising and a well-conceived plan will ensure that your corporate and foundation program succeeds and makes the best use of its resources.

Launching a New Corporate and Foundation Program

If you have been hired to launch or enhance a corporate and foundation program, here are a few hints:

Review current and past donors.

Because making a gift signifies an interest in your institution or one of its programs, previous donors may be some of your best prospects for future gifts. You'll need to identify other prospects from a comprehensive directory of corporate and foundation grant-making programs; these are published annually or available on the Internet, for example through the Foundation Center. (See Chapter 3 for other examples of using technology to research and organize information about prospects.)

Compile a list of local and national corporations to research.

Identify those capable of making a gift. If they are not already affiliated with your institution, determine whether they can be cultivated and a relationship formed. By studying their giving history in light of your institution's strengths, you can develop a list of the best prospects and get to work immediately.

Do your research.

This is a must. Before you call a giving officer, read everything the organization has published about giving priorities and how it prefers to be approached. Review lists of grants funded or study its IRS 990-PF tax return. The benefits of doing this homework first are multiple: You won't waste time and effort approaching the wrong funders; the often-overworked program officer will appreciate not having to read published guidelines to you over the phone; you'll find that future phone calls will be willingly accepted. And above all, you'll create a professional image for your institution.

Start cultivating.

Don't make the mistake of waiting to cultivate prospects until you have thoroughly analyzed your entire prospect pool. You will gain valuable insights from your initial contacts that will shape your developing plan.

Don't expect too much.

Finally, don't rely on corporate and foundation funding for all your institution's needs. Though the money you raise may be substantial, a corporate and foundation program is only part of your institution's overall fund-raising plan, often the part that matches what these entities want to fund. The programs they support will be new and imaginative, projects that differentiate your institution from the rest. You'll need to look toward the alumni annual fund, major gifts, government grants, and institutional funds for long-term support of existing programs.

Developing a Successful Corporate and Foundation Fund-Raising Plan

AT MANY INSTITUTIONS, THE CORPORATE AND FOUNDATION PROGRAM is just one part of a development office in which the major focus is individual giving. Corporate and foundation fund raising, however, requires different strategies from individual fund raising, and developing an organized plan will enhance your ability to secure grants. A formal plan will help you identify which activities are likely to produce the greatest impact and ensure that expectations for the program are realistic.

Many excellent models of strategic planning are available. At Washington University School of Medicine, we use the Guaranteed Fund-Raising System developed by Dennis J. Murray. Its first step is an assessment—to match internal capabilities with external opportunity. This provides the basis for setting realistic objectives, identifying areas of success where effort should continue, uncovering weaknesses to address, tracking trends and anticipating threats, and assigning resources where they will produce the best results.

Analysis of the internal environment involves assessing staff skills and experience, resources allocated to the program, and performance of the program in relation to its objectives.

The external environment includes the number of prospective donors and other characteristics, such as how these entities relate to grant seekers, how they make funding decisions, and how often you can submit proposals. Note any personal connections between your institution and the organization, especially at the board level. Also critical are your relationships with other campus departments that affect your program's ability to achieve its goals. Finally, you'll need to examine external forces such as public policy and the performance of the stock market.

Both the assessment and the development of a fund-raising plan should be carried out by or substantially involve the staff expected to implement the plan. Murray believes that such bottom-up planning creates ownership of objectives and motivates the staff to accomplish them.

Naturally, actions likely to result in increased giving should have the highest priority.

Thorough analysis of the internal and external environment will let you identify specific strengths and weaknesses. It will provide a solid basis for setting objectives that are attainable with your current staff and budget. Moreover, it will identify areas that could produce results if you had additional staff or resources.

Once the analysis is complete, devise strategies to address issues uncovered during the assessment. These strategies form the basis for specific program objectives. Each objective carries a series of detailed action plans that spell out what is to be done, the deadline, and the person or people accountable.

Naturally, actions likely to result in increased giving should have the highest priority. Allocate staff and resources to activities with the greatest income potential.

Implementing the plan will require mechanisms to track results. A personal computer database is essential for regularly reviewing the progress of prospects from identification to solicitation to grant. Tracking will ensure that nothing falls through the cracks and that efforts are focused on the best prospects with the greatest capacity and inclination to fund your institution.

The fund-raising plan is not a static document. Revise your analysis and objectives annually, and revise or drop individual action plans at mid-year to keep the focus on activities with the greatest potential.

The Importance of Understanding Institutional Priorities

MANY INSTITUTIONS ENGAGE PERIODICALLY IN FORMAL STRATEGIC PLANNING to evaluate strengths and weaknesses and to plan for the future. Faculty, administrators, students, and external reviewers all participate. This ensures that the assessment and plans are realistic and a consensus is reached on what should be done. Difficult choices must be made if the financial needs of existing and proposed programs exceed the institution's ability to support them. In a series of controversial and widely publicized decisions during the 1980s, academic departments and even entire schools of colleges and universities were closed when careful analysis indicated a poor prognosis or lack of sufficient resources to support a high-quality program.

Why is institutional planning so important to development? First, it will save you time and effort learning about your institution and gleaning its unique characteristics, both prerequisites for soliciting corporations and foundations. Unless you know your institution thoroughly, your efforts will be hampered by a lack of focus and an inability to distinguish your institution from other grant seekers. Second, with set priorities, you'll have a clearer picture of the relative importance of various needs. Finally, donors are more receptive to supporting an institution that has a clearly defined mission and sound plans for attaining leadership in one or more areas. If you submit a proposal that is consistent with a plan to achieve excellence in that field, a foundation is more likely to view the investment as wise, favoring it over a project that appears tangential to your institution's stated goals or one that looks the same as other projects.

Even if your institution's strategic plan is five or more years old, reviewing it is a first step in familiarizing yourself with the institution you represent. Updating such a plan for fund-raising purposes is much simpler than updating it for academic-planning purposes. Regular discussions with your institution's leaders will keep you abreast of priorities and ensure that fund-raising objectives are consistent with institutional goals. Because the stature of academic programs depends heavily on the faculty, the departure or arrival of distinguished instructors can sometimes shift priorities, either temporarily or permanently. Students are another key factor; declining enrollment can lead to a change in status.

Balancing Institutional Priorities with Faculty Needs

EVEN WITH A THOROUGH KNOWLEDGE OF INSTITUTIONAL NEEDS, your ability to secure support for the priorities identified will depend on the willingness of your donors to support them. Despite their worthiness, the best-laid plans do not necessarily attract support. This is especially true for foundations and corporations, which may narrowly define their funding preferences and may not accept proposals that fall outside of them.

Because of the donor-directed nature of corporate and foundation giving, most institutions seek such support for both priority and nonpriority projects to maximize potential income. With clear direction from your chief development officer and the results you obtain in the first few years of your fund-raising plan, you will find the right balance for your institution.

Balancing institutional priorities with individual faculty needs can be more challenging. At a small institution, you may be able to organize every faculty member's grant search with thorough research, cultivation, a beautifully written proposal, and excellent stewardship. Most corporate and foundation professionals at large research universities quickly recognize that such comprehensive service is impossible to provide for all projects. Allocating staff to every faculty proposal could mean sacrificing your focus on institutional priorities or promising service you are unable to deliver. With a formal plan approved by your chief development officer, you will have greater leverage in setting limits. This will let you establish a reasonable level of service to faculty and avoid striving to be all things to all people.

Beware of projects that have no champion among the faculty or institutional leaders. If the development office is a project's staunchest supporter, what will happen to it when it's funded?

With a reactive strategy, for example, you might suggest prospects to faculty when they seek assistance, provide guidance on approaching funders, comment on draft proposals, and secure a letter of institutional endorsement. Some institutions ask faculty to fill out a form about the proposed project and obtain their department head or dean's signature of approval. Requiring a brief project description can sift feasible projects from unfocused ideas and show you where to invest staff effort. It is important to develop an internal clearance committee to monitor, assign, and approve funding projects and institutional initiatives and match them with funding prospects.

Over time, helping faculty grant seekers will win you friends as word of success spreads. It also leads to greater acceptance of policies related to prospect clearance. You can't control what your faculty members do, but you can establish a few rules that respect the policies of your donors and protect them from unwanted multiple solicitations. This will nurture your long-term relationship with grant makers and create a professional image for your institution. Because program officers talk among themselves, you may find that you reap benefits beyond your current prospect pool.

Project Leaders: The Need for "Ownership"

WHEN A PROJECT IS MATCHED WITH THE RIGHT FUNDING SOURCE, designating a project leader is a critical step. Usually the choice is obvious. But in complex projects, such as those in which multiple schools of a university are all stakeholders, it isn't always clear who will be ultimately responsible for preparing the proposal and ensuring success.

Beware of projects that have no champion among the faculty or institutional leaders. If the development office is a project's staunchest supporter, what will happen to it when it's funded? The development office can be the driver for proposals to individuals, but corporate and foundation projects are different. Just because a foundation funds projects in widget design doesn't mean your faculty will agree to design widgets. Identify the stakeholders before you expend too much effort. The willingness of faculty to help is an excellent signal of either strong support or trouble.

Once the project leader is identified, designate a point person who will keep the project moving. The leader and participating faculty may provide materials for preparing a draft, but someone needs to research the prospect, obtain necessary approvals, communicate with the funder, assemble the final proposal, organize the site visit, and follow up after a grant is made. Having the point person in your office is a real plus, if staffing allows. Occasionally, the project leader will balk at this arrangement, but most will appreciate advice that improves the likelihood of funding.

Seeking Funding for Basic Science Research

APPROACHING CORPORATIONS AND FOUNDATIONS FOR SCIENCE FUNDING requires a strategy different than does soliciting humanities support. For science projects, faculty are closely involved in proposal writing and may serve as the primary contact with the prospect. While both corporations and foundations support scientific research on campus, they require quite different approaches.

In the early 1900s, foundations were the principal supporters of science in the United States—but when the federal government became the major funder of research after World War II, foundations cut back. Today, only 4 percent of the $19.5 billion awarded each year by foundations goes to science and technology.

When you approach foundations that support science, understanding the review process will help you target your proposal to the appropriate audience. While some foundations use a peer-review process to help them identify the most worthy proposals, the program officer and the board that will approve or deny funding are usually lay people.

Foundation proposals must strike the right balance—making a technical project understandable to a layperson but offering sufficient detail to pass muster with scientists. The more fundamental the research, the greater the challenge of communicating its importance to a lay donor. Press releases and feature articles written by your institution's public relations office can provide well-written material for use in letters of inquiry, proposals, progress reports, and stewardship. Building strong relationships with this unit will yield great dividends for your institution.

> Today, only 4 percent of the $19.5 billion awarded each year by foundations goes to science and technology.

Corporations are in business to make money, not give it away. In sharp contrast to foundations that seek to invest in leaders in a field, corporations are not interested in supporting research because it is excellent or because your institution is preeminent. Instead, they fund research that fills gaps in their own capabilities, expands a body of knowledge that will advance a strategic business interest, or allows them access to researchers and even to intellectual property that may arise from the research.

For these reasons, many grants from health-care and technology corporations are contracts rather than gifts or grants. Companies and universities often use the term "grant" with different meanings. A contract clearly outlines what the company expects in return. It may set milestones that must be met by a specific date, give the company certain rights to resulting inventions, or request a delay in the publication of findings.

Corporate research funding usually comes from a research and development unit or even a marketing division rather than the company's foundation or contributions program. It almost always arises from direct interaction between a faculty member and a company scientist rather than from a grant application sent to the company by a development office. The proposed research must fit strategically with the company's business interests, which may be quite narrow.

If your faculty are looking for corporate research funding, encourage them to spend time with company scientists who attend their presentations at scientific meetings. They should also accept invitations to give seminars for companies. By doing so, they'll learn the company's interests and get a chance to show what they can offer. Consulting is another effective avenue for meeting corporate decision makers.

Unsolicited proposals sent to a company generally do little more than provide free, unpublished information. The company can profit from the ideas of your faculty without providing any funding for the research. Work with your technology-transfer staff to ensure that intellectual property is protected when submitting proposals.

Whether the funding you win comes from a foundation or a corporation, it may accrue to another unit's bottom line. Keep your institution's interests foremost, and avoid competing internally for credit. Being large and compartmentalized, research universities generally have multiple contacts with the funder during the life cycle of a grant. Keep the lines of communication open to avoid misunderstanding. Seek a partnership with your sponsored research office rather than establishing and defending territories. Eliminating any trace of overlap in responsibilities is counterproductive and may be impossible. Difficulties also may arise when the research office views its mission as fund raising rather than faculty support. Make it one of your key objectives to develop a mutually supportive relationship.

Seeking Funding for the Arts and Humanities

FOUR OUT OF FIVE FOUNDATIONS SUPPORT PROJECTS IN ARTS AND CULTURE, a sure sign that funders understand the importance of the humanities. Local corporations, too, can be passionate about enhancing the cultural environment of their communities. However, humanities grants tend to be smaller than science grants. The difference is more likely to reflect the expense of specialized facilities, supplies, and equipment for scientific research than the relative value funders place on these two pursuits.

Museums and other cultural institutions get the lion's share of U.S. arts-related philanthropy. Although support for humanities programs is decreasing, a strong case can be made for supporting them at educational institutions. Colleges and universities provide a critical link to the future through the transmission of knowledge to new generations. They bring a special richness to the local arts environment through a continuous influx of students, art exhibits, performances, and visiting faculty. Also, the quality of teaching is greatly enhanced when instructors are active as writers, artists, and performers.

Support for interdisciplinary studies is a growing trend in humanities funding. Women's studies and African-American studies, for example, transcend the traditional departmental structure and allow new ways of thinking to flourish. Technology also is becoming a focus for humanities funding from corporations and foundations. The explosive growth of the World Wide Web and the availability of digitized documents offer students unprecedented access to research materials once available only from special collections.

While scientists can tap a wealth of federal dollars that dwarfs private spending, the humanities also have a special opportunity for government support. The National Endowment for the Humanities offers challenge grants that can multiply the level of support obtained through private philanthropy. Grantees are required to raise three or four dollars in new or increased gifts for every federal dollar offered. State humanities councils, which operate in all 50 states, may offer competitive grant programs. The National Endowment for the Arts is another possibility.

To build support for the arts and humanities at your institution, focus on humanities-oriented grant makers and local donors, and take advantage of government programs that leverage private dollars.

Evaluating the Success of the Corporate and Foundation Program

WHAT IS THE RIGHT MIX OF QUALITATIVE AND QUANTITATIVE MEASURES for determining the success of your fund-raising plan? Should the corporate and foundation program be evaluated differently than individual giving programs?

Evaluating the success of a corporate and foundation program is not the same thing as evaluating the efforts of its staff. Murray believes the primary focus should be on deciding whether program objectives were met, identifying reasons for any failures, and developing strategies to address them.

Most of us are evaluated, at least in part, on the amount of money the corporate and foundation program raises. The bottom line is the most important measure of success, but it is not the only one. Also important are activities that build long-term relationships with donors, sharpen faculty capacity to secure grants, or promote collaboration between development and related departments.

Many of the common parameters for measuring productivity are flawed. Some institutions measure the number of proposals submitted, the percentage of proposals funded, and the number of personal calls made on giving officers. But each of these quantitative measures, especially if a quota is set, can drive staff toward activities that detract from the primary purpose.

For example, proposals that have little chance of being funded should not be submitted simply to pad the numbers. Tracking the percentage of rejected proposals could discourage risk-taking that may result in funding. Requiring a certain level of staff travel also is counterproductive, as many giving officers do not take personal calls. Although generating numerical data is cumbersome for activities such as stewardship or service to faculty, these activities often provide more value to your long-range fund raising. Focusing on achieving realistic goals is the best way to evaluate the success of your corporate and foundation program and guide future efforts.

Trends in Corporate and Foundation Funding

WHILE FOUNDATIONS ARE GIVING AT UNPRECEDENTED LEVELS, cash gifts from companies are declining. However, both corporations and foundations are becoming more directive in their giving. Rather than reacting to needs in the community, they are developing strategic plans and focusing on areas where they can have a real impact. As guidelines narrow, it may be harder to match your institution's needs with donors' goals.

Development staff commonly use the term "enlightened self-interest" to describe what drives corporate philanthropy. Because an educated workforce is essential to employers' future, some companies are focusing more of their support on elementary and secondary education. Similarly, some corporate foundations that used to make grants nationwide are now focused on their local community. This provides the biggest public relations impact for the company and serves its need to develop future employees.

"Partnership" is another buzzword among corporate and foundation fund raisers. Foundations are putting their heads—and sometimes their money—together to accomplish more than any is capable of doing alone. For example, more than 100 of the nation's medical research funders gathered recently to identify areas on which foundations can have the greatest impact. Similarly, grant seekers who work with other organizations to accomplish a common goal can sometimes develop a more compelling case than 5 or 10 proposals submitted separately. Consortia can bring administrative headaches, but their cooperation often allows them to undertake projects that would be impossible for a single institution.

Foundation assets grew significantly during a long period of stock-market growth in the 1990s. Grants are approaching $20 billion as we enter a new millennium. The number of private foundations doubled between 1980 and 1998. New foundations will continue to form as the post-World War II generation ages and the anticipated $10-trillion intergenerational transfer of wealth occurs. Corporations will continue to challenge campuses to propose projects that merit their investment. Long-term relationships with program officers will be key to coping with the threat that mergers and acquisitions pose to corporate fund raising.

Planning is critical to place your institution in the best position to seize opportunities and address threats as they arise. By regularly assessing your internal and external environment and developing appropriate strategies, you can direct your efforts toward activities that produce the greatest impact.

REFERENCES AND ADDITIONAL RESOURCES

Foundation Center. *Arts Funding: An Update on Foundation Trends.* 3rd ed. New York: Foundation Center, 1998.

Foundation Center. Foundation Giving: Yearbook of Facts and Figures on Private, Corporate and Community Foundations. New York: Foundation Center, 1999.

Murray, Dennis J. *The Guaranteed Fund Raising System.* 2nd ed. Poughkeepsie, NY: American Institute of Management, 1994.

Peck, Martha and Susan Fitzpatrick. "Medical Breakthroughs for Sale," *Foundation News and Commentary* 40, no. 5 (September/October 1999): 26-27.

Pew Charitable Trusts.*Strengthening Health Research in America: Philanthropy's Role.* Philadelphia: Pew Charitable Trusts, 1998.

Weeden, Curt. *Corporate Social Investing: The Breakthrough Strategy for Giving and Getting Corporate Contributions.* San Francisco: Berrett-Koehler, 1998.

Your Board: An Essential Partner in Corporate and Foundation Fund Raising

Kevin J. Doody
Director of Corporate Relations
California Institute of Technology

5

Effective board involvement in fund raising is as diverse as our institutions themselves. Whatever form it takes, however, your trustees and others responsible for oversight are essential partners in your corporate and foundation development efforts.

To best capture the value of board involvement, carefully allocate development resources to identify fund-raising opportunities for its members, and then find appropriate ways to involve them. This will help lead to effective and satisfying results for both the board member and the institution.

For the purposes of this chapter, board members are defined as those serving on the institution-wide board of trustees. However, the same techniques and procedures apply to people who hold other oversight positions, such as on an advisory/visiting committee for an individual school, department, research center, or fund-raising campaign.

This chapter focuses on specific techniques to help make your board members effective fund-raising partners. With these techniques, you can discover matches between board members and institutional priorities and ways to use those matches to fulfill your institution's needs.

Know Your Trustees and Let Them Know You

THIS RESPONSIBILITY CUTS TWO WAYS: As a corporate and foundation fund raiser, you need to know your board members, and—just as important—you need to find a way to let them know you. These are not easy tasks. Board members are traditionally, and appropriately, best served on an ongoing basis by the president's or vice president's office. Because board members are chosen for their leadership, influence, and capabilities, they require special support to maximize their value to, and participation with, your institution. Serving the ongoing needs of this group is beyond the scope of this chapter and outside the day-to-day responsibilities of most corporate and foundation fund raisers. However, board members are a tremendous resource for you.

> Knowing the board should be a straightforward activity that involves conscientious follow-through.

Regularly review the biographies of all board members, and have your research office keep the bios up-to-date. This, combined with your understanding of evolving institutional priorities, will help you find possible matches between trustees and needs. Whether this review occurs at special board-member review meetings or during other staff meetings, it will help the staff remember key details in a trustee's biography, including current and past employment, board membership at other companies or foundations, expressed or demonstrated interest in particular campus activities, and so on. When a potential match is found, you must then devise a strategy to involve the board member and have this strategy approved by the president's or vice president's office (see next section). By regularly reviewing all board members, you will avoid the trap of knowing just the most active, and you will spread the potential workload from this often demanding constituency.

Knowing the board should be a straightforward activity that involves conscientious follow-through. But how can the board get to know the fund-raising staff? Development administrators should have the confidence in their staffs to have them make presentations to board members annually or semiannually. Most boards have a subcommittee that deals primarily with development activities; this may be the most appropriate audience. The purpose of these presentations is to explain the goal/mission statement of each development office (corporate relations, foundation relations, major gifts, gift and estate planning, etc.), to demonstrate the services each office supplies, and to give examples of recent or ongoing solicitations. This will help educate board members about the tools they can use as they serve your institution.

A Match Is Found—Now What?

THE PURPOSE OF THE BOARD-REVIEW MEETINGS and staff presentations is to help identify board members whose employment, philanthropic associations, or other connections can make them advocates for a particular institutional priority. When you find a potential advocate, your job is to create an involvement strategy that passes muster with his or her prospect manager, usually the vice president of advancement. Working closely with the president and provost, the vice president may already have a solicitation strategy that incorporates a more strategic, "big-picture" solicitation. If your strategy competes with the more strategic one, this may simply be a case of unfortunate timing. On the other hand, your strategy could be an attractive way to further engage the board member with the institution.

This is also the time to consider realistic resource allocation. When evaluating different board members, you'll need to decide which deserve individual attention from the vice president and which can be delegated to a senior corporate or foundation fund raiser. There are numerous variables at play here, and each decision should be made on a case-by-case basis.

The vice president of advancement can advise on each trustee's personal characteristics as well as the quality of the relationship between the trustee and the institution. Some trustees will be ready to provide immediate assistance; others will need more time to consider their involvement. Some will want to know all the details of a particular project, perhaps even meeting with the involved faculty members. Other board members will be more comfortable writing supportive letters or helping to make introductory telephone calls.

Informing Trustees: How Do They Learn About the Priority Fund-Raising Projects?

SOME INSTITUTIONS ARE FORTUNATE ENOUGH to have a standing board committee that focuses on development questions in particular or institutional relations in general. Many times, these groups are composed of self-selected trustees who have an intuitive understanding of fund-raising challenges and enjoy helping to guide the institution's involvement in the community at large. These committees' mission statements often specify responsibilities such as recommending fund-raising policies and programs and overseeing progress, activities, and solicitations of special importance.

As part of an annual reporting cycle, this committee should receive a progress review and a projection of development priorities for the coming year. Presenting this information to your board demonstrates that your activities are guided by the institution's priorities and allows you to invite members' input and participation. This will help prepare them if a corporation or foundation signals to a board member an interest in a fund-raising solicitation.

Green Light! Board Members Adding Value to Development

ONCE A BOARD MEMBER'S PROSPECT MANAGER okays your involvement strategy, there are many ways to engage him or her in your fund-raising efforts. Listed below are some suggestions for involvement, each supported with specific, real-life examples. The rich variety of possible approaches depends on your creativity, your board member's commitment to the project, and, to some extent, lady luck.

Brainstorm with your board member on an approach.

He or she can provide valuable advice on how a corporation or foundation is structured, how decisions are made, individuals key to the decision-making process, evaluation criteria, and likelihood of success. For example, one institution wanted to ask a corporation for a major equipment donation. A board member familiar with the company knew that it had to purchase many of the components of that equipment from outside vendors; the equipment was relatively more expensive for the company than units manufactured in-house. This insider information helped the fund raiser better understand the company's constraints and so structure a better proposal.

Encourage a board member to write the cover letter or make the call.

A cover letter or phone call from an influential board member helps distinguish your inquiry or proposal from the hundreds of competing requests, especially when it also introduces the corporate or foundation fund raiser. With this introduction, you can start building your own relationships and exercising your persuasive abilities.

Organize a meeting, on campus or off, between the board member and the potential funder.

The board member can invite decision makers to a meeting, perhaps at her own home. If appropriate, involved faculty and students can also participate. In one example, a board member organized an introductory meeting with the CEO of a targeted company. Although the board member had been retired from the company for some time, he had hired the current CEO some 30 years earlier.

Encourage board members to visit corporations or foundations.

Personal visits to prospects are one of the strongest demonstrations of board support of your institution and project. Ideally, both the board member and the president or provost make the call—and, if possible, you attend as well to ensure proper follow-up. Briefing the board member for the

Ronald J. Kraus, president of the New England Colleges Fund, writing in the CURRENTS article "The Changing Face of Corporate Giving" (Feb 1998), notes in his experience the three best ways to approach corporate donors:

■ *Board to Board.* It's always best if the relationship between your campus and a company starts at the board level. Corporate leaders consider interaction with the board of trustees paramount. If you work toward gaining corporate support through influential board members in concert with your top leadership, you're much more likely to receive the attention you need.

■ *CEO to CEO.* One tactic we've used to engage the CEO directly is what we call Presidential Leadership Funds. The president of the corporation gives the president of the campus a direct gift for budget relief and to facilitate action on relevant issues on campus. Some find face-to-face interaction appealing and give these essentially unrestricted gifts accordingly.

■ *Student Involvement.* Another successful strategy is to make students a part of your gift solicitation. Take them with you when you meet with prospective donors, or, when you bring donors to campus, have students talk about a project they're working on.

appointment is the same as briefing any senior manager: He or she will need clear goals for the meeting, strong and persuasive speaking points, a thorough history of the institution's relationship with the target organization, and the ideal "next steps" for the meeting's end. Try to present and discuss this information in person. Some board members will appreciate a rehearsal of the meeting; others will not.

Facilitate special events that board members host or attend.

Board involvement strengthens a special event for all who attend. Design this involvement to strengthen board members' commitment and connection to your institution. For example, a corporate CEO was invited to give the keynote address at a technical conference on campus. This constructive involvement certainly played a role in his later decision to accept board membership.

Invite board members to chair fund-raising campaigns.

This avenue of involvement immediately satisfies two important goals: It strengthens a member's commitment to the institution, and it helps ensure campaign success.

Conclusion

BOARD MEMBERS ARE ESSENTIAL PARTNERS in your corporate and foundation fund-raising efforts. To maximize effectiveness, stay aware of members' employment and philanthropic history, and continually compare this information with evolving fund-raising priorities. Once a potential match is found, create an involvement strategy and have it approved by the board member's prospect manager, usually the vice president of advancement. The best strategies will strategically strengthen the board member's involvement with your institution and tactically accomplish your immediate fund-raising goal. With the steps suggested in this chapter, you can demonstrate to board members the valuable services your office can provide to help them accomplish their goals.

Proposal Writing for Corporate and Foundation Support

Robin Torbron-Warde
Director of Corporate, Foundation, and Academic Support
Brown University

6

It's 4:40, and you interrupt a staff meeting to take a phone call from a trustee of your institution, a liberal arts college. The trustee recounts a casual conversation with the president of a foundation where he learned that the foundation has the resources to increase its giving to colleges outside the region (like yours) significantly. The foundation president seemed to like the idea your trustee presented for a new program at your institution. An unspecified six-figure gift was broached. The trustee reminds you that the deadline for proposals is five weeks away.

What's Next?

LET'S ASSUME YOU WERE LUCKY, and the idea the trustee presented was not new. Maybe it's not the highest priority of your liberal-arts college, but you had talked about instituting this program because of student interest. Plus, a five-week deadline is a luxury.

Before writing and submitting the proposal, you must do two things. First, discreetly verify the foundation's continued interest in hearing from your college. This isn't second-guessing the trustee— just covering all the bases. Let's say you find the foundation president slightly less enthusiastic than your trustee but still encouraging. He invites you to submit a draft prior to the deadline. This is good news.

What's next? Look at the whole picture first. Maybe you are still spending grant monies from a previous year. A quick look at the budget shows a small balance. The staff member in charge assures you that the final expenses are in the pipeline. Still good news. With the luxury of more than one professional in your office, you are able to assign another person to prepare the narrative stewardship report, tally the final budget, and submit it. Now the stage is set for a new proposal.

This is not the only way prospects are uncovered or new proposals generated, but it points out the importance of having trustees who are alert to opportunities and familiar enough with staff to know whom to call with news in a timely fashion. It is equally important that trustees know institutional priorities, so they aren't out there promising proposals for new programs not within the scope of the college's mission.

As the key staff member, you must know your institution inside and out—whom to call, how to access information (such as the budget), and what your institutional priorities are. Next, you must know your funders. In some cases, trustees will help identify donors; in others, you will uncover them through research. In most cases, you will want to make face-to-face contact with a prospective donor. You can accompany your president or provost on a visit to discuss proposal themes—or visit yourself to vet ideas. In either case, personal contact will ensure that deadlines are understood, expectations are kept in check, and your proposal represents the interests of both your institution and the funding source.

Electronic and Paper Prospect Research

LET'S STEP BACK. You are setting up your institution's corporate and foundation office. There is no need to start from scratch. Even if Midwest College has never dedicated a staff member to corporate and foundation operations, your institution certainly has a track record of support. Who gave it? When? How much? What or who made it happen? These are the first entries in your prospect database.

How do you learn about your core prospects and continue to add more? Comprehensive directories used to be mainstays of any corporate and foundation library. Now many institutions prefer the Foundation Center's searchable PC-based CD-ROM. An associate membership allows you to phone the Foundation Center library for information on grants and copies of 990s (IRS forms that all U.S. foundations must file). If money is tight, try your regional Foundation Center for information on corporations or foundations that fund nationally or regionally.

Other electronic and printed data are at your fingertips—even if your budget is small. First, get on the Internet. Almost all corporations and many foundations now have their annual reports online. A key-word search will turn up press releases on grants to other institutions.

Next, check local publications. In most cities, monthly business journals cover corporations. You can do a similar search for foundations that support education. Your campus library may have access to Lexis/Nexis, a database that lets you search recent publications. Though you'll still peruse hard copies of newspapers and newsletters, you will gather more and more information online. Like the *Chronicle of Philanthropy,* most publications have searchable databases at low or no cost. All you need is a computer and a Web browser.

Finally, many college corporate and foundation offices have developed Web sites of their own with subscriptions to major newsletters, databases, and links to applications and guidelines. Though subscriptions can be costly, these searchable databases offer the most comprehensive way for faculty to research their own grants. Ask colleagues at comparable institutions to rate their satisfaction with a variety of searchable database sources.

Making Preliminary Calls for Corporate and Foundation Support

OKAY. YOU'RE TRACKING PROSPECTS, and you've identified several potential funding sources. You know their guidelines and deadlines. In many cases, this is all you need to develop a proposal. However, when possible, you should try to make contact with an individual at the foundation or corporation. As long as you're not on a fishing expedition, a face-to-face meeting or even a phone conversation with a program officer can make the proposal process more specific and more personal.

If the foundation has a two-step process, prepare the preliminary letter and submit it as directed. Most foundation officers will give you feedback by phone that will inform your preparation of the full proposal.

When pursuing large, multi-interest foundations, try first to have your president or chief academic officer meet with the foundation's president or executive director. In that arena, foundation officers are interested in your institution's major projects, distinctions, and challenges. In rare instances, you may find out about a new direction the foundation plans to pursue or convince it to fund a pilot project at your institution.

Don't discount the importance of meeting with foundation and corporate donors at regional and national meetings. In these impersonal venues, you may be able to ask tough questions or find out specific information that will inform a later visit or phone call. At the very least, you can present your card, then follow up with a letter thanking them for their presentation and summarizing a project you are thinking of pursuing with them.

On the surface, most corporate giving priorities may not seem to fit your institution.

Corporations require a different approach. On the surface, most corporate giving priorities may not seem to fit your institution. Several factors are at work, and you need to explore all the angles. Of course, your job is easier if members of your board are leaders of local or national corporations. Or maybe your president is on the board of a regional bank. You will want to seek their advice about an approach and follow their lead.

For other corporations, build your case around the three Rs—recruitment, research, and region. Because corporations tend to recruit on chosen campuses, see how many of your alumni work at a particular firm, at what level they are supporting the institution, and whether any are in a position to help you gain access to the company's contributions arm. This last step can often be achieved only through a visit with that graduate or two.

Your chances of support are measurably strengthened if you also have one of the other Rs in place—research or region. For example, a large telecommunications company may be willing to support a project at a college with a strong engineering or computer-science program. A bank may support institutions with a financial-management curriculum. Or a pharmaceutical company may support a nearby college that can provide summer interns or employee continuing education. Talk to faculty about their contacts. See where your graduates are finding jobs. Visit them to learn about the corporate culture of their employers. If you have enough ties in this multifaceted relationship, your proposal will have a greater chance of success.

The last step in building a corporate relationship is to be realistic about what it will fund. Will supporting your project gain it recognition? Will that project meet the needs of your institution? Read on to find out.

Faculty/Development Office Production of Proposals

THE CORPORATE PUBLIC AFFAIRS DIRECTOR likes your idea for a community-service internship program. Who writes the brief proposal? Who signs the cover letter? Wait! Whose idea was this program anyway?

Let's be realistic. Some funders will not fund your highest priority, whether it is scholarships, a building campaign, or faculty support. Be flexible, but don't create a new program just to get a grant. Say your campus does have an active community-service agenda. More than half your students receive financial aid, and most rely on summer earnings to meet their personal contribution requirements. A program that combines your desire to place students in social service organizations and their need to earn money is a win-win proposition. Combine that with corporate or foundation support, plus the recognition the funder receives for helping both the student and the community, and everyone is a winner.

The theme here: Know your institution's priorities. If you don't already have one, convene a monthly meeting of the president, provost (chief academic officer), vice president for advancement, director of development, and corporate/foundation staff to review and assign prospects and priorities. This process can be formalized as a clearance committee. Your prospect database will produce monthly reports on strategies, proposals pending, grants received, and stewardship. Regular discussions make it easier to develop themes for funding, respond to requests with the strongest proposal possible, and combine the experience of several professionals into clear next steps.

Not all proposal ideas will come out of your committee. Faculty will have ideas; funding agencies will invite you to respond to their initiatives. However, a monthly grants discussion will let you assign priorities and decide which initiatives are worth your time and effort. Figure 6-1 shows the flow of proposals through the institution.

Figure 6-1 Proposal Routing Diagram

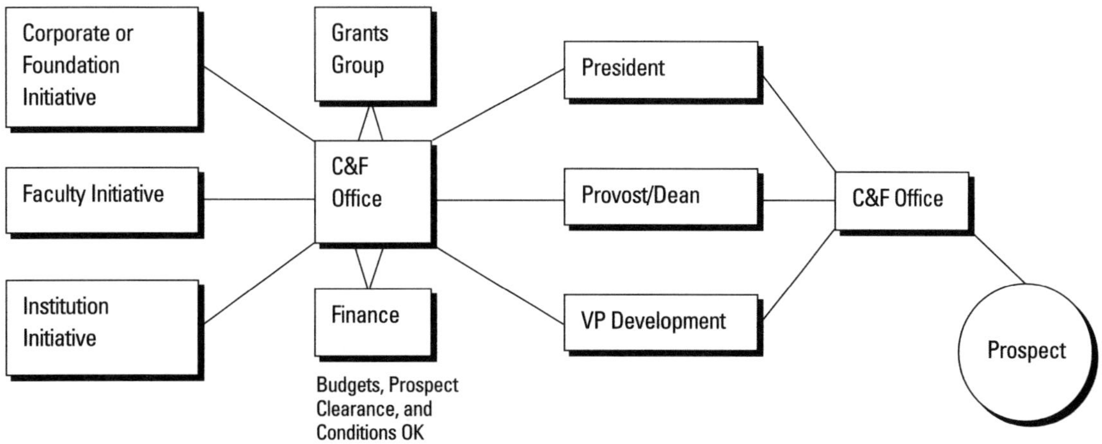

(Credit goes to Ronald Margolin for developing a similar flow chart for use at Brown University. This version was developed for Wheaton College.)

Your responsibility as corporate/foundation officer is to make sure that you are leading with your best fit for a particular prospect. Whether you are the principal writer depends entirely on your institution and resources. Allow yourself time to get input from a variety of sources, but reserve the right to be the final editor, along with the president and provost if they are so inclined. Ask for assistance from faculty and administrative colleagues whose programs will benefit from the grant; set deadlines and follow up. However, chances are you will have to do the bulk of the research and writing and carry out the final submission.

Strategies for Proposal Submission

THERE ARE MANY STYLES FOR SUBMISSION, and most funding agencies provide explicit guidelines. When they are available, always follow them, as they simplify the program officer's job of reading through possibly hundreds of submissions. If there are no guidelines, follow a fairly simple formula:

- cover letter
- introduction or executive summary
- brief institutional background
- outline of project and significance
- institutional qualifications; assurances of readiness and potential success
- plans for evaluation and follow-up

Both the cover letter (signed by the appropriate person within the institution) and the introduction must outline your case succinctly, including the amount of your request. Don't keep the reader guessing!

Stewardship

CONGRATULATIONS! YOU'VE BEEN FUNDED. It's your first grant from XYZ Corporation, and the check is in the mail. Make sure appropriate acknowledgment letters are sent, usually from the president. Next, take a look at other players. Did a key trustee help you gain access? If so, send her a letter outlining your success and thanking her for her role. Keep her apprised of the next steps. On campus, celebrate by sharing the good news, providing kudos to key helpers (the researcher, the administrative assistant, the mailroom clerk). Talk to your communications staff about a press release, which always should be reviewed by the funding agency. Decide whether the grant warrants a story in a publication for alumni, parents, and friends.

If this is an institutional initiative, make sure a project director is assigned and that responsibilities for spending the grant are clearly understood. Review the budget and see that everything is clear. Depending on the funder's requirements, plan for annual (or more frequent) stewardship reports. If someone outside your office will prepare these, give that person clear guidelines, and have the reports routed through your office. If multiple people are involved in spending a foundation grant, it's often easiest for your office to collect the various reports and prepare one final stewardship report. Make sure your report ties in to the goals set forth in the original proposal, and don't be afraid to point out areas that didn't achieve objectives or had unexpected outcomes different from those you expected.

A personal visit can be a part of the stewardship process. Foundations that regularly fund your institution may be willing to visit campus and talk about past grants. During this visit, you can sound out possibilities for future support.

Stewardship closes the gap with the funding source and often paves the way for future grants. Plan ahead, and throw your hat into the ring again after an appropriate wait. If the funder had a good experience the first time around, chances are it will be willing to fund your next project.

SECTION II

Corporate Funding Issues: Strategies for Support

Strategic Corporate Alliances: The Importance of Internal Institutional Collaborations

Michael J. Brennan
Executive Director of Corporate, Foundation, and Research Relations
University of California, Los Angeles

7

During the past few years, there has been much discussion among universities and corporations about how to maximize their relationship so each benefits from what the other has to offer. For some research universities, this has led to development of *strategic corporate alliances*—intellectual, research, and philanthropic activities—with industry that lead to gifts, grants, contracts, and "people exchange." Besides research and philanthropy, these activities also include student recruitment, public affairs, vending relationships, curriculum development, and executive education.

Traditionally, separate offices have handled the individual elements of these relationships. Now central corporate and foundation relations (CFR) offices are becoming focal points for organizing, coordinating, marketing, and optimizing campus corporate relations programs.

The central CFR office can serve as a faculty, department, and school advocate, developing productive collaborations with corporations and increasing corporate support. This model allows an efficient and direct means to help corporations that wish to expand their relationships and to maximize contacts across campus.

Because each institution is unique, it is important to develop a model that encompasses many aspects of interaction between corporations and universities as well as the many ways institutions are organized. At UCLA, for example, the central CFR office works with the offices of the vice chancellor for research and the vice chancellor for administration to coordinate these corporate alliances.

In organizing your approach to corporate fund raising, consider establishing an internal working group whose members represent the operational areas that oversee all aspects of the campus's relationship with a company. This builds on a key element for any central CFR office, the ability to develop and maintain positive working relationships with colleagues campuswide.

Alliance Building and Communication

A WORKING TEAM OF SENIOR MEMBERS from the CFR office, research, and central administration can be most effective in facilitating communication across departments. These departments represent many of the campus areas where corporations have interests, including sponsored research and technology transfer, career services, vending and business services, and philanthropy. Some purposes for such a team:

- *To stay informed.* Information each team member gains from interacting with the company can be useful to others in their own discussions with the company. Perhaps a dean or department has decided to create an industry advisory board to help develop or implement a specific project, say the technology infrastructure of a new academic complex. If the CFR office knows these plans, it can bring corporate partners to the table as stakeholders in the project.
- *To maximize corporate connections.* Many individuals interact within a campus community and within a corporation. CFR's corporate contacts may be key alumni employees, academic relations, and corporate contribution officers. The sponsored research office works closely with the corporate research division. Central operations or administration contacts are historically in sales and marketing. Sharing information on such contacts presents opportunities for building advocacy for campus support across the larger corporate structure. For example, colleagues working on vending contracts with a strategic-alliance company may have information regarding new product lines or brand opportunities. This knowledge may open doors to discussions by CFR or unit development officers regarding event sponsorship.

  Benefits of information sharing can occur on the corporate side as well. Companies often have no built-in mechanism for the marketing, research, community relations, and sales teams to discuss how they, as a corporation, are working with a specific institution. Regularly sharing this information with corporate contacts is a service to them as well.

- *To increase funding opportunities or cross-campus initiatives.* By sharing with colleagues what you learned about corporate strategy and funding interests, you have a much clearer indication of what cross-campus initiatives are possible and how to present them. You will then be able to develop a comprehensive plan that interconnects campus activities, and your corporate contact can help shape that plan within his or her organization.
- *To enhance faculty acceptance and participation.* As your faculty members realize the benefits of cross-department collaboration, they become more willing to strengthen the campus-corporate relationship. Using resources gained by working in teams, you'll be able to help faculty plan proposals and identify prospects for extramural funding, engage federal and state agencies, and report on results once the proposal is funded. Young faculty usually find this especially helpful, and department chairs will appreciate and trust your work.

Using resources gained by working in teams, you'll be able to help faculty plan proposals and identify prospects for extramural funding, engage federal and state agencies, and report on results once the proposal is funded.

Senior-level teamwork sets a strong example to others. It leads to a better understanding of and respect for the roles each office plays and of the benefits of information sharing for increasing everyone's effectiveness.

Cross-Education

SIMPLY IMPROVING COMMUNICATION AMONG DEPARTMENTS and units does not ensure seamless development of corporate alliances. Because this model has the CFR office facilitate the mutual interests of the institution and its corporate partners, it must actively promote cross-education so that all participants become more informed and ultimately serve as better advocates. For example, just as most sponsored research officers have little exposure to prospect cultivation, solicitation, and stewardship, most development officers know little about technology transfer or clinical trials. The CFR staff should attend workshops, conferences, or training sessions on the mechanics of these areas—and should teach the staff of sponsored research and other administrative groups about its focus with industry.

Likewise, strive to educate (or cross-train) faculty members on the roles they play in the success of a broad corporate relationship. Rarely does a company fund a university because of a staff relationship. Rather, funding is based on faculty expertise, an institution's strength as a business resource, or a larger strategic marketing campaign. Cross-education in the basic elements of the total partnership can make each participant a more valuable contributor.

Internal collaboration keeps everyone informed, maximizes the use of corporate connections, increases opportunities for cross-campus initiatives, and enhances faculty acceptance and participation. Therefore, internal collaboration is essential for successful corporate alliances.

Branding Opportunities for Education Support

Larry D. Lauer
Associate Vice Chancellor for Communications and Public Affairs
Texas Christian University

8

Competition for students, dollars, and visibility has led to new ways of looking at marketing higher education in this country and abroad. Every day it is becoming more and more commonplace to hear discussions of concepts such as integrated marketing, relationship marketing, positioning, and competitive advantage on campuses around the world. Indeed, two of the hottest current topics in college and university marketing are branding and partnerships.

In fact, brand name development is usually the mutual interest of most partnerships. And in the case of colleges and universities, it is important to realize that their partners have the same interest as they do in terms of an agreement. And, in addition, when the nature of the partnership is actually a sponsorship, the university will enjoy the extra benefit of a new source of income.

Becoming a Brand

ALL ORGANIZATIONS AND INSTITUTIONS TODAY want to be better recognized as a market segment leader, or as a brand. This is true in both the profit and nonprofit sectors. It is common knowledge that brand names usually have the edge in the marketplace. Most consumers feel more secure and comfortable with a known product or institution and will prefer it over and above the unknown. It seems that what is true for most categories of enterprise is also true for higher education.

This is especially true today. "Baby boomers" are certainly brand conscious, but today's teens, Generation Y, as reported in the February 1999 issue of *Business Week*, are "poised to remake the brand universe." Not only is this younger generation even more impressed by brands than the older generation, but also they are constantly responding to new ones. And so, there is good reason to believe that the better known a college or university is with this generation, the more they will want to attend. The challenge for higher education, then, is to determine how to build brand names.

David Aaker, in his book *Building Strong Brands,* lists the basic elements of a brand. They are:

- The qualities, uses, and values of products or services,
- The attributes and culture of the organization itself,
- The personality of the products, services, and organization, and
- The visual and heritage symbols used to stand for both.

Brand equity, then, is largely built around the emotional benefits perceived in association with these other elements.

In order to manage the brand's development, a variety of strategies must be employed—especially since so many elements of brand must be addressed. One of Aaker's favorite examples is Saturn, where the slogan has become, "sell the company, not the car." Its values, employees, and even its special kind of customer become the component parts, which constitute the perception of the brand. These emotional concepts plus awareness, perceived quality, and the right associations become critical to achieving competitive advantage and customer loyalty. And it is this last very important aspect of building brands, "associations," that has led some colleges and universities to the idea that impressive partnerships can be an extremely effective strategy in the overall branding of the institution.

Our conclusion, then, is that for a college or university to become a brand, it needs to become highly visible in selected higher education market segments... so visible that the institution's name alone stands for the best of its category.

Forming Partnerships

FOR MOST NONPROFIT INSTITUTIONS, and most especially for colleges and universities, one quick way to get visibility is to form a partnership with another highly visible organization. It can also bring new prestige, and, as noted earlier, sometimes even new income. If the organization is well known and respected, additional visibility for both partners can be almost immediate. This is because such projects often are well reported by the news media. But even more, the public seems to have a higher degree of notice when two organizations come together for some good cause or purpose.

Indeed the benefit goes both ways. For a college or university, the visibility is immediate and it conveys a message of community involvement and relevance. It says, "we are an important corporate citizen," and each time that message goes out, brand name development moves ahead one more step. And in the case of sponsorships, the income to the university can even become annual. For the other partner organization, the visibility and branding benefit can be significant enough to improve product sales, customer relationships, and loyalty.

Branding opportunities exist for smaller institutions much the same as larger ones. The key is to find mutual interests that can be enhanced through a cooperative venture. It is a matter of aligning strengths you have with strengths they have and developing a compelling proposal that looks doable to both parties. These ideas can be tied to any credit or noncredit program in the institution, i.e., arts, human services, technology, communications, public education, leadership development, health services, academic conferences, issues workshops, social action projects, etc.

Brand advancement is high on everyone's list of motivations for getting involved.

Ideas can come from anyone in the institution. Many will come from advancement professionals once they begin to look for them. Others will come from professional school faculty, athletics staff, continuing education people, and so forth. But as in major gifts fund raising, after the idea has been developed, the best way to get organizations together is through their CEOs. In other words, your president can propose the partnership to theirs. This is important so that the eventual partnership can be announced as a really significant enterprise.

Actually, college and university partnerships can be formed with many kinds of organizations... corporations, museums, arts organizations, human services, health organizations, cities, governments agencies, associations, other educational institutions, and more. In some cases, the university may get the larger visibility lift, but in all cases, the other organization stands to significantly enhance its prestige and positioning in the community. Brand advancement is high on everyone's list of motivations for getting involved.

Examples of Good Partners

The best partnerships are those where the other organization's business also benefits. Here are some examples.

Seton Hall University. This New Jersey institution has formed an alliance between its School of Diplomacy and International Relations and the United Nations Association of America. This partnership gives the university immediate high visibility in the field of international studies in the United States and abroad. The UNA has 26,000 members and 66 affiliated organizations worldwide. In announcing the alliance, Seton Hall President Monsignor Robert Sheeran said, "Our alliance with the UNA-USA ensures Seton Hall of attracting top students from around the world, and, upon their arrival, will provide these students with a very powerful program of education and experiential learning."

Texas Christian University. This university in Forth Worth, Texas, formed a partnership with its city and KERA-KDTN public television to host an international public television conference. This partnership enabled the organizations to attract more than 800 public television producers from 37 countries to the city, exposing the city to these TV producers, enhancing the public television stations' professional positioning, and giving TCU contacts all over the world for its media students and faculty.

As an additional example, TCU's School of Music recently became an "all Steinway" school. This move, made possible by a generous donation, put the university's piano program on a short list of very prestigious schools, and qualified it to be included in numerous Steinway promotions and activities.

University of Georgia. Delta Airlines and the University of Georgia award an annual prize that recognizes efforts to advance international understanding and cooperation. The Delta Prize for Global Understanding is presented to individuals or groups whose initiatives have promoted peace and cooperation among cultures and nations. The award is presented at an annual ceremony in Atlanta, which attracts scholars, diplomats, businesses, and cultural leaders. The Delta Airlines Foundation gave UGA an $890,000 grant to establish the program. The grant is used to provide a $10,000 cash award and an original work of art to the winner and to conduct the award ceremony. As a global airline, Delta sees its business interests enhanced when intercultural understanding is improved. And UGA benefits from the branding visibility provided through press coverage and through Delta airlines' worldwide communication activities. The proposal for the program came from UGA's Center for International Trade and Security and its Center for Humanities and Arts.

Georgia Tech. The Georgia Tech Athletics Association has a unique multi-million dollar sponsorship/marketing partnership with McDonald's Corporation. Under the sponsorship agreement, McDonald's operates two restaurants on the Georgia Tech campus, both featuring a Georgia Tech décor package. As a part of the sponsorship, an area on campus, which includes the sports coliseum, is named the McDonald's Center, and the McDonald's name is placed on the basketball court, tickets, and other materials. In addition to the significant financial support, Georgia Tech benefits from the visibility resulting from the partnership.

Penn State. Penn State and Pepsi have forged a $14 million partnership. The partnership will fund critically needed facilities and programs, and Pepsi has primary scoreboard advertising rights in the convocation/events center and the football stadium, as well as exclusive rights for marketing Pepsi products on 21 Penn State campuses and managing vending services at the University Park campus. This is an example where facilities have been funded outside the traditional fund-raising approach, and yet both the institution's interests and the company's brand name benefit.

Other Partnerships/Sponsorships

The new world of digital and Internet technology is opening a whole new array of partnership possibilities. For example, publishing textbooks online seems to be the wave of the future, but keeping students from pirating materials remains a problem. Houghton Mifflin, the Follett Corporation, and the State University of New York at Buffalo have partnered to launch a "digital rights management" software feature to solve the problem.

Hundreds of colleges and universities have signed up commercial companies for advertising or other services on their Web sites. An example is Appalachian State University, where students find ads from dozens of companies when they check their email or course outlines on line, including Amazon.com, Dell Computer, and an apartment locator service called SpringStreet.

The possibilities for partnerships of all kinds now seem endless in a field where not long ago they were few and far between. Opportunities exist with almost every kind of organization, from private real estate developers to environmental conservation associations.

Cause-Related Marketing

Sharing a cause is also a good premise on which to explore partnerships with other organizations, profit and nonprofit. Increasingly, corporations are interested in partnerships or sponsorships that promote a cause, especially when that cause is related to a special interest of theirs. For example, Maxwell House Coffee has sponsored a number of Habitat for Humanity home building projects. At TCU, a special freshman orientation program was linked to this project, and the resulting high visibility was beneficial to all parties.

This high interest in promoting the common good related to issues—issues in health, environment, human services, public education, the arts, and more—provides a wonderful opportunity for educational institutions to link with high-visibility, prestigious, outside organizations. Sometimes the partnership is between two institutions, and sometimes it is a partnership between a program inside the college or university and an outside organization.

For example, schools of education have "adopt-a-school" projects. Programs in journalism have partnerships with newspapers. Social work programs have relationships with human service agencies. Obviously, there are many more examples. The point, however, is that when the interest is mutual and the prestige and visibility of the partner is high, not only are these agreements significant for program substance; they are also significant for building the brand name.

Conclusions

THE MARKETPLACE OF HIGHER EDUCATION is changing. Effective marketing practice is becoming essential to be competitive in an increasingly complex environment. But, marketing is a way of thinking, not necessarily a way of commercializing. And building brand equity by establishing effective associations and partnerships is one very effective strategy.

REFERENCES AND ADDITIONAL RESOURCES

Aaker, David A. *Building Strong Brands.* New York: The Free Press, 1996.

Ind, Nicholas. *The Corporate Brand.* London: McMillan Press LTD, 1997.

McKenna, Regis. *Relationship Marketing.* Reading, MA: Addison-Wesley Publishing Co., 1991.

Harris, Thomas L. *Value-Added Public Relations.* Chicago: NTC Business Books, 1998.

International Corporate Fund Raising: Taking a Global View

F.A. Hilenski
Director of Development, Ivan Allen College of Liberal Arts
Georgia Institute of Technology

9

Unlike domestic corporate development, which maintains a semi-autonomous niche on most American and Canadian campuses, international corporate development is normally more integral to an institution's overall international development initiative. Thus, in attempting to outline the best practice for seeking support from international corporations, it is useful to review milestones in the brief history of international development in general.

After World War II, a growing stream of European universities and other organizations began to travel to the United States for fund-raising advice. In the United Kingdom (UK), such interest peaked in 1981, when the Thatcher government's changes in the funding formula for British universities prompted the Council for Advancement and Support of Education (CASE) and the UK Conference of University Administrators (now merged into the Association of University Administrators) to present a three-day conference at the University of London's Bedford College on income generation for universities.

The 60 participants in this conference organized by John G. Kelly (then Bursar at Bedford, now head of Brakeley Europe) heard from such CASE notables as James L. Fisher (then CASE president), Robert G. Forman (then executive director of the University of Michigan Alumni

Association), John Kuhnle (then CASE vice president for management, now managing vice president of Korn/Ferry), and Colette Seiple Murray (then vice chancellor for development at the University of California-Irvine and CASE chair, now CEO of Paschel Murray). This gathering proved a key stimulus to the British universities represented, many of which later set up development or alumni offices of their own.

The perceived success of these institutions, together with increasing pressure from the Thatcher/Major governments to diversify funding sources, led CASE to sponsor in 1990 a development institute at Edinburgh University. More than 100 participants—some not even officially hired—represented the full spectrum of British higher education. American advancement officers and staff members from the handful of British institutions then actively doing development served as the faculty.

What transpired was a remarkable attempt to translate American fund-raising methodology into terms that fit the British higher educational system. During a session on program organization, for example, Warren Heemann (then chair of the CASE Board of Directors and an early champion of CASE's international agenda) would pause periodically to allow his British partner, Colin Boswell (then director of development and alumni affairs at the University of Kent at Canterbury, now director of CASE Europe), to interpret his remarks for his British audience—a protocol that lent credence to Churchill's observation that the United States and Great Britain in reality are two countries separated by a common language. Be that as it may, the Edinburgh CASE Institute proved a great success, and CASE Europe now sponsors an annual institute in Edinburgh as well as many other conferences and seminars throughout Europe.

To understand the fundamental reason American campuses do international development, you must approach the question strategically rather than logistically.

Over time, such transatlantic encounters led to a growing awareness among North American fund raisers that the techniques they had developed for American and Canadian universities could also be applied to non-American settings as well. By 1996, there was enough interest for CASE to sponsor its first-ever domestic conference on "International Fund Raising." Convened in Washington, D.C., this conference generated many more questions than answers, as only a handful of American institutions were actively practicing international development at that point, and virtually none could point to any significant results, much less offer up models of best practice. Still, by reinforcing the efforts already under way and emboldening more campuses to take the plunge, the conference had a real impact.

In 1998, CASE's second conference on international development—chaired by Scott G. Nichols, development dean at Harvard Law School, and significantly retitled "Fund Raising from International Constituencies"—took the international development initiative to the next level. Rather than try to cover the field in general, the 1998 conference narrowed the focus of inquiry to professional practice and provided case studies drawn from the institutions that had begun to emerge as leaders in this new field.

A third CASE conference, held in Seattle in 1999, demonstrated the rapid development of this new field. Again led by Dean Nichols, the faculty featured a veritable who's who of international practitioners from both sides of the Atlantic and from the West Coast and Asia. From Europe were

Adrian Beney, deputy director of development and alumni relations for the University of Durham (UK) and John G. Kelly of Brakeley Europe. From the University of Toronto came Vice President and Chief Development Officer Jon Dellandrea (and a 1998 CASE presenter) and Associate Director of Development Avon MacFarlane. In addition to Dean Nichols, the U.S. faculty consisted of Ronald V. Margolin, vice president for development and director of fund raising at Brown University (who had taught at the 1996 and 1998 CASE institutes) and Julia Hsiao, director of international development for the University of California, Berkeley. Together, faculty and participants at the 1999 CASE conference developed an outline of current best practices in international development, including those specifically related to international corporate development.

In the remainder of this chapter, we will first describe these best practices, and then attempt to outline various roles corporate development can play internationally. This overview should allow you as the proponent of international development to begin an international development initiative at your institution as well as understand how international corporations in particular can contribute to this endeavor.

Rationale for International Development

THE FIRST QUESTION THAT YOU AS THE INTERNATIONAL DEVELOPMENT PROPONENT must address is, Why do international development at all? Or, in the words of Scott Nichols, "What gifts can you possibly get from a trip to Paris that you couldn't get quicker and cheaper from still another visit to St. Louis?" Though this question makes sense in terms of most development officers' practical intuitions, it actually misrepresents the issue at hand. To understand the fundamental reason American campuses do international development, Nichols and others emphasize that you must approach the question strategically rather than logistically.

In June 1993, *Policy Perspectives* reported on a yearlong Pew Trusts-sponsored "transatlantic dialogue" among 24 educational leaders and scholars from central and western Europe and the United States. The report stated that dialogue participants had come to the conclusion that a single fundamental proposition and its principal corollary describe the world of the modern university:

- "Proposition: The changes most important to the university are those that are external to it. What is new is the use of . . . market forces to reshape the university.
- "Principal Corollary: The failure to understand these changes puts the university at risk. The danger is that the university has become less relevant to society precisely because it has not fully understood the new demands being placed upon it."

Perhaps the most significant of these market forces is the increasing demand for universities to contribute directly to economic growth and development. Economies and markets have become increasingly global, particularly since the end of the Cold War, and American corporations have responded by becoming global as well. American colleges and universities, however, are only now beginning to understand that they too must operate in and contribute to this global economy or risk lessening if not losing their societal relevance.

Moreover, with more than 500,000 foreign students studying annually in the United States, and millions more now comprising a significant portion of the intellectual/economic/political elite in their home countries, American institutions have an unprecedented opportunity to seek support internationally. Results of early efforts to date are, in fact, impressive. Princeton University, for example, recently announced a $100-million gift from Hong Kong financier Gordon Wu. Cornell has quietly accumulated more than $100 million over the past decade from Irish philanthropist Charles Feeney. Japanese donors have funded 32 chairs at MIT over a 20-year period. Indeed, both strategically and tactically, American institutions have no choice but to raise funds internationally. As Scott Nichols puts it, "If your institution is not doing international fund raising, you can be certain that your competition is."

Principles of Best Practice

THE 1999 SEATTLE INSTITUTE ARTICULATED A NUMBER OF PRINCIPLES of best practice for international development. First, before any plans are made or visitations scheduled, an institution should "internationalize" its organization and support structure. In particular, it should create a database of international alumni by country, with profiles of any who are already donors, and internationalize its boards, councils, alumni events, and publications.

Then, because international development is practical only when focused at the country or city level, institutions should identify a region, country, or city to focus on by matching research or program areas with alumni distribution patterns worldwide, making particular note of the following:

- Concentrations of prospects and donors;
- Concentrations of alumni and friends;
- Venues of academic collaborators;
- Sources of high-quality potential students;
- Relevant constituencies (e.g., wealthy people or companies with no institutional connection who might give to benefit to country or city); and
- Economic/political/legal conditions affecting potential donors and students.

Institutions should also locate such concentrations and conditions geographically: "Literally, I put pins in a map," Jon Dellandrea says. Then, before scheduling any overseas visits, they should develop a case or mission statement for foreign financial support and publish it in the language of the country or countries targeted. They might even consider establishing a separate advisory board for international outreach, either for the program overall or more preferably by targeted region.

Next, in evolving an action plan, development officers should incorporate the following principles of practice wherever relevant.

- *Follow the money—go where the best prospects are.* Research all institutional and personal connections with a targeted region/country/city, and disseminate information to all relevant parties. Convene knowledgeable faculty and staff to advise on each targeted country. Track overseas visits by senior faculty and administrators, and determine whether any visit should be at least partly prospect-driven. Prepare relevant profiles, itineraries, and briefing books for every such visit.
- *Recognize that international fund raising is built more on quid pro quo dealings than on relationships, at least initially.* An individual, for example, may want his or her gift to support a student from the donor's region, family, country, or city. A foreign company, if sponsoring a program, will want to know how many (free) admissions it will get to distribute. Realize that, without a clear "win" for the donor in the arrangement, an international initiative is likely to fail. Thus, at Harvard virtually every dollar raised from foreign sources goes initially to support students, faculty, and programs of the donor country. Quid pro quo is also manifest in the various elements of cultivation—e.g., introductions, attention to visitors, gifts, hospitality, and the like. Ultimately, of course, the goal is to get international donors to support institutional/academic priorities regardless of parochial focus, but getting there usually requires a gradual widening of perspective through education and involvement.
- *Remember, however, that relationships still are critical to long-term success.* At the end of the day, people give to people. In an international context especially, gifts come out of relationships, which must be selectively established and carefully maintained. Though institutions may be hesitant to plunge into international cultivation activities in a country or region where it feels it lacks "expertise," in actuality relationship-building overseas need go no slower than relationship-building domestically.

The entire CASE faculty of the 1991 Institute agreed that, generally speaking, waiting until a college or university has hired an expert in the region or mastered the culture is a waste of time, opportunity, and money. In reality, the quality of the institutional case typically will rise above mere cultural insensitivity or ignorance. While one should always minimize cultural *faux pas*, most nationals are willing to make allowances for lapses in decorum or behavior as long as one's motives are transparent and sincere. For this reason, it would be a mistake to "go native;" institutionally, says Nichols, "you should be what you are—i.e., an American university, with all that implies with regard to mission, demographics, and culture." Toward that end, Harvard makes a point of including Jewish and women faculty in its delegations to the Middle East.

In building such relationships, remember, too, that keeping a paper trail is essential: advance letters, case statements, thank-you letters, memos-to-file, contact reports, all gain added importance in maintaining an institutional memory of a relationship that may span several turnovers of development personnel. Attention to details like correct titles, addresses, and phone numbers also takes on heightened significance in an international context. And in communicating with international prospects and principals, fax is best for ordinary correspondence, though e-mail is beginning to replace it. Senior officers or officials, however, will not respond to e-mail; electronic traffic should therefore be routed through their assistants.

- *You will be known by the company you keep.* Identify and recruit on-site guides, organizers, and advocates who are preferably high-status loyalists or opinion leaders (e.g., distinguished professors, business or governmental officials). Indeed, in the initial stages of international fund raising at least, perception is as important as action—so opinion leaders are as important as decision makers.
- *Establish a physical presence; be perceived as having made an investment.* Build on existing activity: Setting up an office is ideal; at minimum, sponsor a local club and make quarterly visits. Move incrementally: The University of Toronto has set aside seven years to "do" Hong Kong; Dellandrea has made eight visits there in 24 months, and his president visits annually. "You can't get major gifts from once-a-year contacts," he stresses. In addition to "chief-of-state" (i.e., presidential) visits, consider other types of visits as well—introductory trips, advance trips, seed-planting and case-making trips, stewardship visits, victory tours. Regular visits to alumni and to the parents of international students are a good idea as well. Consider hosting a major event—a kickoff or presidential visit—at least biannually. UC-Berkeley, for instance, sponsors a regional conference in Asia each year, always in a different country and locally sponsored. If you decide to mount such a conference, seek local sponsorship to underwrite costs, and have your local host handle invitations and RSVPs.

To garner gift support, try offering this carrot to local supporters: You would like to bring your president or dean but cannot without something on the table, for to come without a gift in place would cause him or her to lose face. Nichols reports that Harvard once postponed a visit until local alumni had identified some form of support. Once on site, take your shots when you can: Instead of visiting a potential donor several times before making an ask (as you would at home), schedule several contacts with a potential donor over the course of your stay, in a variety of venues and social settings, culminating in an ask. Finally, try to find ways and reasons to bring foreign alumni and friends to campus and, once there, arrange for them to make multiple contacts.

Corollary: Do not raise false expectations—for example, show up once, make a big splash, promise to return, and then fail to show up again for five years. Such behavior is worse than having no presence at all. And too, American institutions need to have a local presence in bad times as well as good. People have long memories: Keeping the faith and continuing to have a presence in a targeted country during a down period is much appreciated and often rewarded, even though the reward may be delayed. For that reason, perhaps the best time to begin cultivation in a country or region is when its economy is down, as in the Pacific Rim in the late 1990s. Institutions seeking to engage in international fund raising need to take a long-term view—three to five years at minimum, five to 10 years ideally.

- *Make a serious financial commitment to your overseas strategy.* "This is not a game for the faint of purse," Dellandrea observes. Think strategically about the expected return on investment, especially local investment (office, staff, club support, etc.) in a target city or country. In this context, the CASE faculty collectively counsels novice institutions to beware of false economies: Choosing cheap hotels, parsimonious food and hospitality, and coach airfare over business class on long trips will all prove counterproductive in the long term. Overall, the CASE faculty suggests an annual commitment of at least six figures. Of the campuses represented on the CASE faculty, UC-Berkeley's annual expenditure of $250,000 marked the low end, while the University of Toronto's more than $1 million (US) marked the high end. "If cost offset is necessary, make it a high priority to identify early on a foreign sponsor to underwrite at least part of these international fund-raising expenses," notes Ron Margolin.

- *Set realistic targets and devise verifiable means of evaluating progress.* Try to adapt the benchmarks and evaluation processes used in domestic fund raising. At the same time, remember that because the goal in international fund raising is strategic rather than logistic, these data must be weighted accordingly. Create appropriately different standards for international development and review them annually.

While international fund raising is a daunting task, the CASE faculty urges development officers not to be intimidated. "The only bad move is to not move at all," says Nichols. "Have a bias for activity and a bias for solicitation"—in other words, when in doubt whether to act, act; when in doubt whether to ask, ask. And as you begin this trip of a thousand miles, Margolin adds, "be guided by the history and culture of your institution."

Corporate Development in International Fund Raising

Corporations and businesses can help with at least three essential tasks in international development: ice breaking, lead giving, and bridging.

Corporations and businesses can help with at least three essential tasks in international development: ice breaking, lead giving, and bridging.

The first and perhaps most critical of these tasks—ice breaking—includes activities such as introducing an institution to the logistics of operating within a foreign country and advising its development operations on the ground. In this context, American international corporations are especially effective. Being American, they are already familiar with the concept of corporate citizenship and, ideally, are participants (if not leaders) in the corresponding culture of giving; as global organizations, they are experienced in overseas markets. Therefore, officials of such corporations can be especially helpful serving on an area advisory council for a targeted country.

Brown University provides a good case in point. Before launching its international fund-raising initiative, Margolin reports that Brown asked advice and support from corporate CEOs operating in its targeted countries. "This move realized a dual benefit," he says; "The CEOs brought us valuable advice and contacts, while we educated them about our international activities and needs for foreign support." Such global corporations can also be helpful in identifying and supporting key employees—particularly alumni—to act as local guides and allowing an institution use of its overseas offices, at least until it can establish a more autonomous presence.

Secondly, international divisions or subsidiaries can serve as patrons of an international initiative, particularly as lead donors. Should a given global corporation have a foundation, support can be in the form of a multi-year grant. Alternatively, the company can sponsor an event locally—a form of giving even foreign-based businesses are quite familiar with and willing to do, so long as their marketing criteria are addressed. UC-Berkeley, in hosting its annual corporate seminar in Asia, finds support for (and thus participation in and commitment to) the seminar through sponsorships from companies with major offices or facilities in the host country.

In addition, many foreign countries make tax provisions for corporate giving, though often the mechanism will not be labeled as such and may, in fact, appear strange or convoluted to American eyes. For example, France reputedly makes no provision for corporate giving. It does, however, allow corporations paying a mandatory taxe d'apprentissage (a training tax) to assign a portion of those payments to approved educational institutions and programs—including those partnering with American institutions. Thus, it might be worthwhile to meet with the tax accountants or attorneys of corporations sympathetic to an international initiative—say, one or more of those serving on an international advisory board—to explore the corporate tax options of a targeted country.

Thirdly, corporations can act as bridges to other sources of support: individual, corporate, and even governmental. Supportive global corporations—or even local or national corporations with foreign suppliers, lenders, or buyers—can also provide access to and leverage with their foreign subsidiaries, partners, and customers. By working with participants in their various corporate affiliate programs, for example, Georgia Tech has been able to attract support from foreign-based global corporations with which their affiliates do business.

Sometimes American institutions can collaborate with foreign counterparts to solicit corporate support via governmental programs that promote university-industry projects. The European Union promotes such projects through both its major research support initiative, the Community Framework Program, and more targeted programs like the Community Action Program in Education and Training in Technology (COMETT), wherein corporations and industries frequently participate as paying partners in consortia involving American or Canadian partners of a European university. American institutions may also work with European institutions to seek such support directly, without the benefit (or restriction) of a governmental broker.

The key to making the case for support in any and all of these scenarios? "It's the quid pro quo, stupid!" Making certain there is something in the deal for a corporate supporter has always been an essential element of successful appeals domestically; it is even more vital in soliciting to support of a foreign-based company or subsidiary.

To keep from losing one's ethical footing in such rocky terrain, remember what corporations are seeking by supporting an institution: to gain access and become more attractive to the best students; to enhance their reputation, credibility, and competitiveness; and/or to acquire usable knowledge. In turn, institutions must be clear about what they are seeking: typically, access to new resources (both financial and organizational), engagement with an influential and potentially strategic organization, and/or acquisition of corporate intelligence and proprietary knowledge.

The trick, of course, is to make both parties happy and eventually to engage the corporation in a long-term partnership that broadens its involvement in and support for the institution. Those that manage to craft a mutually satisfactory relationship with an international corporation usually achieve, of course, increased funding. But just as importantly, they also develop through this partnership a strategic orientation that is essential to their long-term institutional vitality and viability—that is, a markedly enhanced ability to contribute directly to the global economy and marketplace, and thus improved institutional relevancy to the demands of an increasingly global society.

Corporate Fund Raising at Large Research Universities

G.A. Hartford
Former Senior Director of Corporate and Foundation Relations
University of Michigan

10

Most large research universities embrace the theory of "every tub on its own bottom"—fostering rampant internecine competition among units and making corporate and foundation relations messy, at best. When your job is coordinating corporate strategic direction for the fleet of tubs, you are lucky to avoid being hit in the crossfire, let alone succeed in moving them forward. In addition to this level of autonomy in the schools and colleges (many with their own well-staffed development offices), the large number of research institutes and centers, each seeking external funding and often reporting to multiple deans, adds a substantial degree of complexity to corporate fund raising.

These inherent characteristics provide serious obstacles to overall university strategic planning and priority setting, which are the heart of a well-defined campaign or fund-raising program for a university. The ambiguity of such a structure makes operating a corporate and foundation fund-raising program more of an art than a science. This chapter will look at special problems for corporate fund raising at large research universities: the relationship with the sponsored research office, contracts vs. contributions, university organizational structure, office procedures and policies, technology and confidentiality, and measuring productivity.

Relationship with the Sponsored Research Office

THERE ARE THINGS YOU LEARNED IN KINDERGARTEN that you really should continue to practice. Holding hands as you cross dangerous intersections remains good advice, even when working with your sponsored research office.

That office typically works directly with individual faculty, helping them raise funds from the federal government as well as foundations and corporations. Its services may include assistance with proposal writing and prospect research through computerized databases such as the Sponsored Program Information Network. Usually an approval form signed by a dean or unit administrator is required before assistance is given. This form requires the faculty member to reveal considerable information about the project or proposal including budget, all sources of funds, use of human or animal subjects, use of carcinogens or other dangerous materials, and space needs.

The sponsored research office has a compliance or enforcement function, and this information is necessary to satisfy that mandate. That office usually also negotiates research contracts with corporations, including intellectual property rights. It is also involved in contracts for clinical trials and material use agreements.

> The need for corporate and foundation fund raisers to work closely with the sponsored research office has led some universities to a dual reporting structure with lines to the chief development or advancement officer and the chief research officer.

In working with this office, you'll have to determine which office processes proposals or gift solicitations for sponsored projects. Sponsored projects are complex, have several sources of funding, and often include federal grants. The sponsored research office must process all proposals supporting such projects. I believe this is necessary to keep the corporate development office focused on raising money and, to be candid, away from many of the time-consuming compliance issues.

At Michigan, these two offices developed a memorandum of understanding that is still a work in progress. We became good partners and even conducted joint training sessions on campus. This cooperative activity is worthwhile in a college or university of any size but critical in the large research university.

Contracts vs. Contributions

THE SIMILARITY OF WORK AND COMMUNITY OF INTEREST between the sponsored research office and the corporate and foundation development office necessitates that they jointly interpret the National Association of College and University Business Officer's *Guide to Distinguishing Between Contracts (Exchange Transactions) and Contributions* (hereafter *NACUBO Guide*). This guide is Appendix D of the *CASE Management Reporting Standards.* They must then jointly work with the financial operations office on university policy to be conveyed to all operating units. I can virtually guarantee infighting between the two offices and rampant misunderstanding and confusion across campus units if the two offices do not reach some understanding on these issues.

A simple agreement on a definition may help classify contributions vs. contracts. At the University of Michigan, the presumption is that all awards from a foundation are voluntary support with donative intent, whereas corporations may make either contributions or contract payments. This important distinction separates the issue of who helps with proposals and processes the paperwork from the more important issue of how the university should record each transaction. In 1988, the university's sponsored research office processed more than $17 million from foundations that were counted as contributions. I made these results known on campus so the sponsored research office received credit for its development efforts.

More and more universities are engaged with large corporations in relationships that have been touted as philanthropic but in my opinion are substantially more contractual. These relationships may be labeled branding opportunities and include long-term contracts with corporations involved in soft-drink manufacture and sales, fast-food service, sports equipment, and others. Many of the agreements are contracts involving a quid pro quo relationship. Press releases announcing these "deals" claim the corporation has made a gift or contribution. That could be a misrepresentation. It appears to me the corporations have generally made a payment to the university in accordance with a long-term contract, and I believe close examination of the *NACUBO Guide* will support that conclusion. These gifts also may have been derived through nothing more than increased costs to student consumers. Duke University has such relationships with multiple soft-drink corporations, but they are nonexclusive, and Duke was careful to solicit and receive substantial contributions from the corporate foundation after the contract was negotiated.

Although corporate development officers may wish to be involved in such discussions, I advise spending time on other, clearly philanthropic activities. This whole arena of corporate branding also involves use of the institution's good name for the corporation's advertising or marketing purposes. Universities may not wish to have their name associated with certain corporations at some point in the future, and many are addressing policies on the use of their good name.

University Organizational Structure

CORPORATE AND FOUNDATION INTERACTIONS are so pervasive throughout large research universities that the reporting structure of having the office report solely to the chief development officer is being challenged. The need for corporate and foundation fund raisers to work closely with the sponsored research office has led some universities to a dual reporting structure with lines to the chief development or advancement officer and the chief research officer. That is the case at Duke, UCLA, the University of Virginia, and the University of Massachusetts.

At the University of Michigan, I satisfied the need for close coordination by creating an alternative structure. A coordinating committee consisting of the provost, the vice president for research, and the vice president for development was established and staffed by an associate from each office. These officers agreed to function as a quasi board of directors for the corporate and foundation fund-raising effort and functioned very well in spite of their rather unwieldy name: the

Executive Officers Corporate and Foundation Coordination Group. This group, focusing on formulating policy and setting priorities, is key to setting the basis for the Michigan program. Our provost is responsible for budget administration and thus was a welcome member of the group, adding great credibility to the policies and decisions. It is essential that these three university officers be involved in setting policies and priorities for corporate and foundation fund raising, regardless of the organizational structure.

Office Procedures and Policies

WE ALL REALIZE THE DIFFICULTY OF PROVIDING FOCUS to corporate development officers and helping them zero in on the most productive prospects. If you are a supervisor, you can help provide that focus with appropriate workload assignments and a clear definition of what constitutes a major gift.

Many universities assign corporate prospects according to geography, as with individual fund raisers, but my preference is to assign prospects according to industry type: automobile, other consumer-durable capital goods, information technology and electronics, aerospace and defense, finance, real estate and insurance, chemical, energy, and health. Your categories should be based on your own list of corporate prospects. Development officers would necessarily be assigned more than one category but would become experts in a limited number of industry sectors.

A clear and most likely expanded definition of a corporate or foundation major gift prospect is also important. At Michigan, to be considered a corporate major gift prospect in the central office, a donor has to be capable of giving $250,000 over five years and have multi-unit relationships. Foundations must be capable of giving $1 million over five years and have multi-unit relationships. If the relationship is with a single unit—for example, the School of Business with finance or insurance companies—the prospect is left to that unit to manage, cultivate, and solicit. This policy recognizes that the central office spends a substantial amount of time coordinating efforts and adjudicating disputes between units of the university. These definitions and limits should be established to fit each institution

Chapter 4 covers program development, but a discussion of coordination and clearance policies is also worthwhile in this chapter. Most policies require that faculty or academic unit personnel clear or receive permission before visiting or soliciting a corporation. The rationale for these policies is usually twofold:

- The central office wants to be sure the amount solicited is appropriate and its purpose is a university priority, and
- The central office wants to avoid the embarrassment of two university representatives visiting or soliciting the same company within a short period of time.

Be certain your policies are well thought out and are focused less on control than on providing information to the central office. There are so many potential corporate prospects that I have never observed the unlikely scenario of a visit by the president followed on the heels of a visit by a dean or other official.

Also recognize, when enforcing a coordination policy, that there is a subtle but big difference between a company's public affairs or philanthropic division and an operating unit. For example, Ford Motor Company has made contributions to the University of Michigan from 25 different accounts, including the Ford Fund (its philanthropic office). I needed to know about transactions with the 24 operating units but did not need to control access to them. I did need to control access to the Ford Motor Company Fund, at its request. Numerous affiliate programs and other research relationships brought Ford personnel into almost daily contact with faculty. Be flexible: These contacts by faculty are very important and, when brought to the attention of the corporate foundation, will help build the case for corporate support of the institution.

Also recognize, when enforcing a coordination policy, that there is a subtle but big difference between a company's public affairs or philanthropic division and an operating unit.

Technology and Confidentiality in Corporate Support

ALL UNIVERSITIES HAVE SOME TYPE OF COMPUTERIZED DATABASE for prospect tracking. Confidentiality policies were often developed with the individual prospect in mind. Data on individual donors must be guarded closely and treated very confidentially, but corporate and foundation prospects are public entities, and data on them is a matter of public record. The exception, of course, is small family businesses like doctors, dentists, and accountants; these may be managed much like individual prospects.

Recognizing this difference has very real ramifications for the large research university, where it is desirable to share data on corporate and foundation prospects with a large number of faculty and fund raisers. This led us at Michigan to develop an intranet Web site with research information on centrally tracked corporations and foundations, including visit data, corporate officers with university ties, primary contacts, gift history, and a link to the corporate Web site. The site is open to all university personnel willing to share information on their corporate and foundation contacts. Users across campus can submit updated information on their contacts with corporations and foundations directly to the site.

The development of our intranet Web site won CASE's Circle of Excellence Leadership award for educational fund raising in 1998. Michigan has high hopes for this site particularly as more faculty and staff become accustomed to using it. Two fundamental premises of the intranet are that prospect research data must be converted to electronic form so it may be readily used by a large number of people and that the data be disseminated broadly to all faculty and staff who can benefit from it.

Measuring Corporate Relations Productivity

MEASURING PRODUCTIVITY IS A DIFFICULT EXERCISE AT MOST INSTITUTIONS and conducted haphazardly at many. Some institutions focus on developing the relationships with corporations, and their criteria measure relationship building through, say, the number of executives on committees, number of research grants, and number of campus visits or presentations by corporate executives. Other institutions measure the activity of fund raisers, including the number of days on the road, number of contacts monthly, number of proposals written, and caseload.

While I recommend monitoring the other data, I prefer to concentrate simply on funds raised. This is, of course, the prime mission of a development officer and of corporate relations. It is best to give program leaders a certain degree of latitude in designing the program and a rather long term of two or three years to begin to deliver results. Given that latitude, the amount of money raised—benchmarked with peer university results—is the fairest and simplest way to evaluate the program.

A good resource is the Council for Aid to Education's annual *Voluntary Support of Education.* Although it contains a wealth of comparative data, its usefulness is diminished by the variance in the reporting procedures used by many universities and colleges. For comparisons to be meaningful, institutions must follow the CASE/NACUBO standards in reporting their fund-raising results. Currently a number of institutions, including some in the top 20, deviate from those definitions.

Conclusion

TRUST MUST DEVELOP between the central office and unit development officers for a truly effective fund-raising program to flourish. These are my top five general tips to directors responsible for corporate fund raising in a large, complex research university:

- Focus on raising money for institutional priorities. Do not let turf considerations, your ego, or the desire to control the process interfere with this objective.
- Strive to develop the best collegial corporate fund-raising atmosphere possible throughout the university. There are numerous corporate contact points throughout the university, and the most meaningful and productive occur with faculty. You need the assistance and cooperation of the faculty and the unit development staff.
- Search for ways to add value to each corporate relationship. If the relationship is focused on one university unit, perhaps you cannot add value and should let the unit manage it.
- Listen and strive to understand the point of view of the unit development officer or faculty member. Worry last or not at all about who receives credit for the contribution.
- Adjust to changing circumstances, be flexible, and avoid rigid interpretation of policies.

REFERENCES AND ADDITIONAL RESOURCES

Council for Aid to Education. *Voluntary Support of Education 1998*. New York: CAE, 1998.

Council for Advancement and Support of Education. *CASE Management Reporting Standard: Standards for Annual Giving and Campaigns in Educational Fund Raising*. Washington, DC: CASE, 1996.

Dermer, Joseph, and Stephen Wertheimer, editors. *The Complete Guide to Corporate Fund Raising*. New York: Public Service Materials Center, 1982.

Shannon, James P., editor (Council on Foundations). *The Corporate Contributions Handbook*. San Francisco: Jossey-Bass, 1991.

Levy, Reynold. *Give and Take: A Candid Account of Corporate Philanthropy*. Boston: Harvard Business School Press, 1999.

Corporate Support for K-12: A Nation at Risk

Kenneth Spritz
Fund-Raising Consultant
Kenneth P. Spritz & Associates

11

The state of America's public schools is a cause for concern. The problems facing our educational institutions are enormous, and their causes are a continuing source of speculative debate. Whatever the combination of potential causes—lack of funding, fossilized teachers' unions, bloated bureaucracies, or lack of parental involvement—it is clear that the institutions providing the basic fabric of our society's welfare and sustenance are in jeopardy.

The title of this chapter implies that a measure of responsibility for the current state of public education rests with the corporate community. Not true: Corporations depend on the outcome of our educational system but bear no more responsibility for its shortcomings than do administrators, teachers, parents, or students. However, the corporate community recognizes its need for an educated and skilled workforce and has finally taken steps to contribute to a solution.

This chapter will examine how industry has responded to this crisis and will attempt to anticipate the future direction of corporate philanthropy and partnership on the basis of historic patterns.

History of Corporate Philanthropy

CORPORATIONS ARE NOT PHILANTHROPIC BY NATURE. Indeed, philanthropy in its purest context cuts against the grain of any company's basic mission: to make a profit. Prior to the 1950s, corporate philanthropy was primarily an extension of the private largesse of wealthy industrialists. The vast majority of early initiatives aimed to benefit company employees or their families directly: housing, recreational facilities, medical care, and the like. In the years between World Wars I and II, these limited gestures were supplemented with annual campaigns for national programs (such as the Red Cross) or local consortia (such as Community Chests).

Following World War II, a few corporations sought to respond to what was then perceived to be a crisis in private higher education. However, not until a landmark legal case in 1951 were corporations allowed to support these institutions where direct self-interest was not demonstrable as a rationale for support. The opinion from this case (*A. P. Smith Manufacturing Company* vs. *Barlow*) is powerful in anticipating our current situation:

> . . . there is now widespread belief throughout the nation that free and vigorous non-governmental institutions of learning are vital to our democracy and the system of free enterprise and that withdrawal of corporate authority to make such contributions within reasonable limits would seriously threaten their continuance. Corporations have come to recognize this and with their enlightenment have sought in varying measures . . . to ensure and strengthen the society which gives them existence . . . .

With this endorsement and legal license, corporations undertook a tradition of support for private higher education. During the 1950s and 1960s, contributions were usually in the form of unrestricted support for endowment or building purposes to the alma maters of senior executives and corporate directors. As corporate giving programs gained experience and engaged professional staff, grants to this group of recipients (expanded to include the top tier of prep schools attended by these same corporate officers) narrowed in their focus to better address the broader corporate relationship with the institution: support directed toward an engineering or business school or scholarship support for minority students, for example. As public universities entered the arena of private fund raising in the 1970s, corporations slowly expanded their eligibility requirements to include these institutions—both for the purpose of public relations and in response to the significant resource they represented for recruiting new employees.

> The broad-based impact of corporate contributions on our society is slight in relation to other forms and sources of giving.

Changes in corporate giving priorities and direction continued through the 1980s in response to greater shareholder oversight and bottom-line consciousness. Unrestricted support of elite prep schools gave way to diversity grants or subject-specific support related to corporate activity or identity. The line between corporate philanthropy and sponsored research blurred as a greater percentage of the corporate dollar was targeted to university activities in which there was a clear corporate self-interest. Similarly, charity and marketing became intermingled as grant support was often considered in relation to the number and brand of either soda machines or computers on campus.

Through this chronology, several interesting trends and themes emerge. First, corporate philanthropy has steadily evolved from a sense of "enlightenment . . . to ensure and strengthen the society which gives them existence" to a highly focused and often self-interested blend of charity and marketing.

Secondly, corporate philanthropy has to a very great extent been reactive rather than proactive. Working within a relatively narrow set of guidelines for prioritizing grant support for institutions (e.g., recruitment relationship, number and position of alumni within the corporation, relevance to areas of research and development, proximity to the campus), corporate foundations' specific program initiatives invariably follow the lead taken by other funding agencies. Private foundations were first to recognize and respond to most of the key initiatives that corporate giving programs have adopted as priorities: support for women and minorities in the sciences, arts education and outreach, democratization of South Africa, AIDS education, research and assistance, to name but a few. Occasionally, a company will venture forward with its own form of program-related investment (such as American Express' Academies for Insurance and Travel) but these too often are in response to a perceived corporate need rather than a societal need.

Finally, the broad-based impact of corporate contributions on our society is slight in relation to other forms and sources of giving: Corporate funding represents only 19 percent of all private support to educational institutions and approximately 6 percent of all charitable donations to all causes. Given that corporations tend to spread their support across a wide array of organizations to cover the broadest range of corporate interests, the impact of any given company or group of companies on a particular broad-based problem is questionable.

Trends in Corporate Support of Education

As corporate giving programs and corporate foundations evolved through the 1980s into the professionally managed operations we know, the crisis facing K-12 public schools appeared as an issue demanding response and involvement. Though few corporations (and only a handful of private foundations) directed their support to the most substantial part of the educational community in the country, the long-term implications for the collective corporate community provided a de facto mandate for involvement.

Unfortunately, recognition of a problem of this magnitude—as with school violence, homelessness, and substance abuse—often leads to debate, blue-ribbon panels, government commissions, and few concrete solutions. Private foundations that have attempted to address the education crisis (most notably the Annenberg Foundation with its $100-million grant) find themselves either throwing good money after bad or accepting that serious, systemic change will require a far longer time and a much more substantively involved relationship than is common.

Nonetheless, corporations have begun to respond. Some have focused their efforts in home-office or operating locations on local school reform that directly benefits employee families and allows for employee/volunteer involvement in the adopted school. Other companies have taken a more systemic approach on a regional, state, or national basis. All efforts should be applauded, but solutions will require a long-term commitment or partnership that may too often be tested as companies review their quarterly balance sheets. The questionable report card on the $100-million Annenberg Foundation grant to reform a number of inner-city public schools demonstrates that money alone won't solve the problems.

Given the historical relationship of corporate philanthropy to education, certain projections can be made as corporations move to include public elementary and secondary schools under their umbrella of support:

- The pool of available corporate money will not significantly expand. Between 1978 and 1998, corporate support to education grew approximately 10 percent per year even while public colleges and universities were widely added as a category of support. There is no reason to expect that significant new resources will accommodate public school support.
- Support for higher education and independent schools will decrease. Certain companies have already taken this step through a restructuring of their giving programs to highlight school-reform initiatives.
- Higher education will, however, continue to benefit—at least on paper—from corporate support targeted to public schools by serving as the conduit or sponsor of educational reform initiatives. Corporations (as well as private foundations and individual donors) are justifiably leery of public schools' or districts' ability to administer their grant funds and manage their own reform programs. In the future, corporations might expect colleges and universities receiving significant ongoing support to demonstrate a commitment to the issues facing public elementary and secondary education.
- Competition for corporate funds will increase significantly as public schools develop their own fund-raising programs. We are already seeing a huge increase in the number of public schools establishing nonprofit foundations on the model of the public colleges and universities. A number of prep schools (most notably the selective, exam schools such as Boston Latin, Brooklyn Tech, and Walnut Hill) have launched or will soon launch capital campaigns. CASE is considering an expansion of its member services to address issues specific to the public K-12 sector. The very definition of the educational community in the context of private philanthropy is undergoing a major alteration.

Who will be the winners and losers? Higher education will clearly continue to receive a high percentage (if not the vast majority) of corporate support given continuing relationships through recruitment, executive education, and research. Those colleges and universities positioned to contribute in a substantive manner to improvements in public schools will share some portion of funds earmarked by corporate foundations for that purpose.

On the other hand, independent schools will likely suffer greatly in the face of public school competition. Although corporations play a relatively insignificant role in the total philanthropic profile of independent schools (according to the Council for Aid to Education, in 1997, corporations contributed $2.6 billion to higher education and only $22 million to independent schools), these institutions will find it increasingly difficult to maintain their levels of support in the face of the compelling case made by public schools.

On a purely financial basis, the real winners emerging from shifting corporate philanthropic priorities will be the public schools. Foundations and corporations will target individual schools or districts for long-term reform and restructuring. Increasing numbers of schools will take a proactive approach to development by establishing their own affiliated foundations, developing annual giving programs, and undertaking capital campaigns.

Whether we as a society benefit from this public/private partnership depends on the results achieved from the undoubtedly substantial resources directed toward this crisis. Without doubt, this is truly an effort to "... ensure and strengthen the society which gives (us) existence."

REFERENCES AND ADDITIONAL RESOURCES

Burlingame, Dwight F. and Young, Dennis, editors. *Corporate Philanthropy at the Crossroads.* Bloomington, IN: Indiana University Press, 1996.

Himmelstein, Jerome L. *Looking Good and Doing Good: Corporate Philanthropy and Corporate Power.* Bloomington, IN: Indiana University Press, 1997.

SECTION III

Foundation Funding Issues: Positioning for Institutional Success

Strategic Planning and Institutional Priorities

Bruce Wyatt
Vice President for External Affairs
Beloit College

12

In my first development position, as a director of foundation relations, the college where I worked received grants in two primary ways. First, because of history, reputation, stature, and good working relationships between the current and past presidents of the college and foundation officials, we were on a number of lists and would periodically be invited (formally or informally) to apply for grants. Frequently, this support was to be directed to a broad area like "humanities" or "the natural sciences;" occasionally, we were advised to request funds for "the college's highest priority." We received a majority of the grants for which we applied.

The second approach involved taking "a really good idea" (as determined by the dean or president), usually developed further by a small group of faculty, and shopping it around to several foundations. While our success rate was lower at this, we were fairly successful, and the funded projects had a positive effect on the college. (Too often there was only a weak plan for institutionalizing the program at the conclusion of the grant period, but that is another story!)

Most readers will by now understand how naive I was and how truly different the world of foundation grant making is since the mid-1980s. This chapter will concentrate not on how or why organizations plan but on how the results of such planning affect grant seeking and grant making. My analysis is based on my own experiences at two national liberal arts colleges over the past 15 years as well as conversations and correspondence with colleagues at seven other liberal arts colleges and one regional and three national foundations, all in the United States.

Matching Plans to Proposals

ALL THE FOUNDATION OFFICIALS I SPOKE WITH stressed the importance of making explicit the connection between a grant proposal and the institution's strategic plan. One reported, "We seek an articulated strategic plan and, if not available as a formal plan, we spend sufficient time interacting with the applicant to feel confident that the project does fit a plan, formal or informal, that takes the organization into the future." Another longtime foundation official commented, "I believe it's essential to have the proposed project be a part of the college's overall strategic plan. Not only does this mean that the program is an institutional priority; it also indicates that careful thought has been given to both short- and long-term goals. It is important to see how the requested project's budget will fit into the overall college budget (and how the project will be funded after the grant runs out)." Clearly, foundations are looking not just to support "good works" but to help institutions break new ground and accomplish articulated goals.

Beyond consonance with a strategic plan, funders look to the internal logic of the proposal itself. One official, noting the importance of "the problem analysis out of which the proposal comes," told me, "Colleges and universities are often not particularly critical in devising programs. . . . We see problem analysis as one of the guarantees that what is proposed will be better rather than merely different." So those seeking grants must understand the problem(s) fully before developing a plan of action. Modifying an existing program or creating a new one merits funding only if the projected outcomes address a clearly identified and well-defined problem.

Similarly, college officials acknowledge the importance of comprehensive institutional planning. Wrote one, "We almost always refer explicitly to our strategic plan. It has been a great asset in fund raising." Another colleague notes, "We've found that foundations (and corporations) want to know that there is a solid plan in place, that we're not just out there chasing dollars without any particular preference as to where or how the dollars are spent."

Strategic plans generally result from significant input from many sources, including governing board members. Interestingly, while all the colleges I contacted underscored the important role the campus CEO plays in foundation fund raising, reaction to provost, dean, or board involvement was mixed. At some institutions, academic leaders and faculty actively formulate and implement foundation grant-seeking strategy. But board members are generally not seen as especially interested in foundation grants or much potential assistance (except, obviously, with family foundations).

There is a general perception among college staff that foundations have become more "professionalized" in the last several decades. This seems to mean that foundations are less likely to make grants largely on the basis of personal relationships (with board members or presidents) or institutional prestige or reputation—and that foundations themselves have engaged in more systematic planning and priority setting.

I asked colleagues in both foundations and colleges whether personal contacts matter in grant seeking. Are grants cultivated, as gifts from individuals are? An official of a foundation that supports a regional set of colleges replied, "Since we know the colleges well and they us, there is some background level of 'cultivation' at all times." Another foundation official notes, "The old saw that we fund people, not projects, has great validity. We are always interested in meeting with the president as well as the staff and administration directly associated with the proposal." Yet another foundation official noted that meetings with presidents or development staff can be a waste of time, as these are seldom the people who will actually carry out a project. This underscores the importance of choosing the right person for each kind of contact—inquiry, clarification, discussion, negotiation, and so on.

While none of the foundations I contacted acknowledged that they had a formal "strategic plan," all made it very clear that significant planning informed the development of program areas and guidelines for proposals. This appears to be true at both the board and the staff level. Frequently, higher education leaders are consulted as part of the foundations' planning processes, through ad hoc focus groups or formalized advisory boards. A number of foundation directors and staff are former college or university presidents, deans, or faculty members.

Limited resources and increasing demand for grants impel parties on both sides to demonstrate that there is a strong fit of priorities.

While some may fear that foundation priorities could drive college decision making, this seems not to be the case. One college executive wrote, "There's nothing worse than getting a grant for a spiffy new program in which there is no faculty interest." Another notes, "Of course, we would be happy to get more support from foundations, but we do not try to create programs simply to get foundation support." Colleges must, sometimes regretfully, decline to compete for grants when the required programs fall outside their areas of interest and expertise. For example, not all institutions of higher education are well positioned to undertake cooperative K-12 programs, a currently hot area for foundation support.

Colleges and foundations clearly stress the importance of planning, whether or not it's a lengthy, formal process resulting in published objectives. Limited resources and increasing demand for grants impel parties on both sides to demonstrate that there is a strong fit of priorities. As a foundation official told me, "If a project is isolated, i.e., if it is the brainchild of a college officer or group of faculty, yet doesn't fit within a strategic or programmatic context and reinforce or extend an institutional purpose, then its life may be coextensive with the enthusiasm of the sponsor and coterminous with the life of the grant." Paying lip service to an institution's long-term commitment to a program is insufficient. Colleges and funders are best served when a grant truly provides start-up funds, not short-term life support.

College officials have long recognized that foundation grants bring both dollars and prestige. Successful foundation relations programs invest time and effort in grant proposals that clearly reflect articulated campus priorities. No institution is likely to claim that all of its faculty and administration agree completely on all aspects of a strategic plan or have a wholly shared vision. Nevertheless, securing significant foundation funding is made easier by a clear sense of direction and of the ways a proposed program or project contributes to it. Presidents and deans must be able to articulate this in broad compass, while faculty members who will implement the grant must explain how details of program components relate to larger goals. Good stewardship begins with clear thinking and a coherent plan to meet an important institutional need.

Foundation Support: Part of a Total Institutional Effort

Patricia Martin
Director of Corporate and Foundation Relations
Carleton College

13

Colleges and universities that regard foundations as just another source of money will miss opportunities to develop the institution and interact with constituents in important ways. An effective foundation relations program does raise money, but its value cannot be measured solely by the annual total of grants received. It also articulates institutional priorities, makes connections with faculty and students, leverages individual gifts, and creates opportunities to enhance the institution and fulfill its mission in new ways.

Effective foundation relations offices look into the institution and out to the world beyond. Foundation relations staff often have more contact with faculty and senior administrators than do their colleagues in annual funds, major gifts, or planned giving. Developing proposals—a much more accurate description than "writing grants"—enables foundation relations officers to work closely with faculty who are shaping projects or programs. In the process, we come to know about their teaching interests, research, and publications as well as emerging issues in their disciplines. By knowing your institution well, you will marshal a wide range of facts to make the case for support: the number of female science majors in the past decade, the most popular majors, the percentage of tenured faculty, the average financial aid award, or new courses and programs offered.

You articulate the institution's mission, the vision of its leadership, and how both enhance learning and teaching.

At the same time, foundation relations officers must understand trends in education, especially as they affect foundation funding. You need to know about current issues and how the institution is responding to such topics as economic efficiencies, collaborations, K-12 partnerships, and workforce readiness. Foundations want to support new ideas or proven ideas in new settings, and the foundation support office is the bridge between these agencies and the institution.

The Value of Leveraging

FOUNDATIONS HELP INSTITUTIONS SECURE GIFTS FROM INDIVIDUALS by issuing challenge grants or grants with matching requirements. Challenges are particularly effective because they require the institution to raise a certain amount of money, often by a specified date. Challenge terms may also include minimum and maximum gifts to be counted, number of donors required, and even donors' past giving. Challenges can create a sense of urgency among individual donors and show that their gifts help secure other funds. Successful challenges also raise sights, encouraging donors to stretch to participate; the result may be sustained individual giving at a level higher than before.

Many foundations recognize the strategic value of challenges. For example, the mission statement of the Kresge Foundation, which makes capital challenge grants, says in part:

> We believe that a challenge grant toward an organization's capital project does more than just build a building or reward good programs. It presents an opportunity to build institutional capacity by helping an organization broaden and deepen its base of support from the private sector and by encouraging volunteer involvement in the fund-raising effort and beyond.

Other foundations implicitly challenge institutions by requiring a commitment to sustain activities initiated with "soft money." These arrangements can also leverage long-term support, often from individuals.

Foundation grants, with or without a challenge component, can provide important validation for the work of an institution—luster that may help attract gifts from individuals, corporations, and other foundations. Even for those closest to the campus, major foundation support sends reassuring messages about the institution's quality and the wisdom of their continued investment in its future.

In recent decades, many foundations have moved from being passive and responsive to being active in grant making and agenda setting. Those that once routinely supported institutional priorities and provided operating support—budget relief—now may see themselves as change agents. Foundations have become active in fostering collaborations and partnerships, requiring program evaluation and assessment, and encouraging dissemination and modeling of successful projects. Foundation relations officers may find themselves balancing the institution's imperative of raising funds for already identified projects against foundations' mission to foster change. And it is often just such external incentives that lead to innovation.

The synergy among foundation grants, institutional innovations, and individual gifts can have a powerful impact on schools and colleges. For example, Carleton established its Learning and Teaching Center (LTC) with the support of the Bush Foundation of St. Paul, which has a special interest in faculty development at area colleges and universities. Assisted by a 1991 Bush planning grant, faculty members held workshops, met with consultants associated with successful centers, and considered both the theoretical and logistical questions surrounding such an enterprise. Near the end of the planning year, we developed a proposal to the Bush Foundation for three years of LTC funding, a grant that was followed by three additional years of support. Along the way, Bush provided consultants to follow our progress on site. Later, with help from a Bush matching capital grant, Carleton endowed the position of LTC coordinator. And, with LTC's value and success evident, an individual stepped forward to endow the center. Generous foundation support created opportunities for the college to establish an important program and for an individual to ensure its future.

> The synergy among foundation grants, institutional innovations, and individual gifts can have a powerful impact on schools and colleges.

Foundation and Corporate Relations?

IN MANY RESPECTS, CORPORATE AND FOUNDATION RELATIONS ARE SIMILAR: Both work with external constituents, develop formal proposals that are evaluated and awarded competitively, generally focus on project-based funding, and typically result in short-term support. Should the operations be combined? It depends. Here are some factors for you to consider:

- *Nature of corporate relationships.* If your institution heavily involves trustees or alumni in corporate solicitations or if you have mostly contractual relationships with corporations, your foundation and corporate staff probably work in very different ways. Corporate efforts may have more in common with major gifts than with foundation programs.
- *Size of shop and volume of grant activity.* Does your institution develop enough grants from both corporations and foundations to require staff in each field? Is the total staff large enough to justify separate reporting lines? If not, one office is more efficient.
- *Need for flexibility vs. need for specialization.* Fund raisers must keep up with their prospects, especially as corporations merge, new corporations form, and giving interests evolve. But it is also crucial to stay nimble, with staff available to take on promising new projects. Can your program keep area specialists productively busy all the time? Are you prepared to forgo some flexibility in order to dedicate resources to each aspect?
- *Budget.* Corporate and foundation relations should be among the most economically efficient fund-raising efforts, reflected in relatively low costs per dollar raised. Look at your total budget for three-to-five-year grant cycles. Over time, can you afford to

staff corporate or foundation support efforts at current levels? Are there nonmonetary returns that justify maintaining both?

Related to the question of one staff or two is *who reports to whom*. Here the models multiply rapidly, with two dominating: having foundation relations report directly to a vice president or dean, and reporting through a director of development, usually along with annual funds, major gifts, and planned giving. Reporting through a director of development makes sense for combined corporate-foundation efforts based on many alumni or trustee connections. But, in many cases, reporting through the director of development adds a level of management to an already top-heavy process. Reporting directly through the vice president or dean reflects the reality that foundation relations is a strategic office with distinctive characteristics and close ties to senior administrative officers.

Like individual gifts, foundation grants are built on relationships. Staff in foundation offices must develop relationships not only with donors but with faculty and institutional leadership and staff. Developing and maintaining these internal partnerships is critical to success. Effective foundation fund raisers manage not only down but also across and up. Skills in managing information, ideas, processes, and people are the most critical in leading an effective, efficient, productive foundation effort. These skills enable us to work with faculty to develop projects, with staff at foundations to ensure a good fit between their interests and those of the institution, and with fund-raising colleagues to meet challenges and matches and to sustain projects over time.

Takin' it to the Street: Raising Foundation Dollars for Community and Regional Programs

Cathy Hanby-Sikora
Principal Consultant
Hanby-Sikora & Associates Inc.

14

It can happen this way: You're a development officer at, say, Arts & Sciences College in Nicetown, USA. A group of faculty come to you on a warm afternoon with an idea. They have dreamed up a new service project, and they're excited enough to invest some of their own time and expertise in it. They believe that, if successful, it could improve your institution's relationship with its community.

It's the age-old "town and gown" issue that, if your college is like most, requires almost constant attention. The institution needs excellent community relationships. So your task is to help the faculty think through its program, decide how to describe it meaningfully to foundation prospects, and find the dollars.

Or it could happen this way: You're a development officer at ASC, and your president wants to showcase faculty talents by providing a greater range of services to your community. It's your job to identify how those talents can benefit your community, drum up the necessary commitment among your faculty, and find foundation dollars to get the program going.

Or it could happen like this: You're still at ASC, visiting foundation officers in your state to find out what they are thinking these days, as you must if you're going to broker good matches between their strategic interests and your fund-raising priorities. The new program officer at Yourstate Charitable Foundation tells you it will soon look for innovative programs that address a specific problem the foundation has identified as strategically significant. Then she says that there hasn't been much meaningful synergy between ASC and Yourstate Charitable Foundation, evidently because they just don't seem to have the same priorities.

You know it rarely works to cook up a program just to attract the dollars. But you also know that the foundation interest she has just identified is important to your president. Now your job is to find a way to position ASC as an institution in which Yourstate could become interested. One way to do that is to identify a program on campus that is ready to be developed and funded, one that you can use to cause Yourstate Charitable Foundation to start thinking of ASC as a potential partner.

In each of these cases, among the first and most important tasks is program planning and development. What does that mean? How do you know when you're doing it? And what are the essential parts? Knowing your programs—and how to describe them to potential funders—is an essential prerequisite to finding foundation funding.

Program Planning and Development: The First Step

LET'S GO BACK TO THE FIRST SCENARIO. What should you think about as you plan a program that can have real value outside Arts & Sciences College and help you demonstrate its value to your community? Here are some questions to consider.

Question 1: What is the problem?

Foundations generally like solutions to a problem that most people *agree* is a problem. It won't work to say, "The problem is that we really need this program." This question is probably the most important part of the planning process because if there isn't a good answer, you generally need not go any farther in your search for foundation dollars. Foundations exist to change something in the world. There is something that has so moved every foundation's original donors or current board or strategic planning committee that it has dedicated its resources to changing it—to solving that problem.

At all costs, avoid describing the problem in terms of your institution's fund-raising goals.

Does your community honestly need what you have to offer? How do you know for sure? Who else thinks so? What kind of data will demonstrate that fact? Who has so much credibility that just a few statements from him or her would immediately cause your funding prospects to take notice? And is the problem not only important and compelling but of a reasonable size and scope? That is, with the people and resources you have available, can you reasonably expect to affect it?

At all costs, avoid describing the problem in terms of your institution's fund-raising goals. I know you hate to have to say it to your faculty group, but foundations aren't generally moved by financial needs—unless a foundation director sits on your volunteer board or fund-raising committee (pay very close attention to those). Stating your needs in terms of society or community is more compelling. (Don't worry about whether your faculty understand this. The organizations that fund their own research do it because they believe the world needs to know the answers that research will produce—not because Assistant Professor Smith needs to get one more grant and a few more articles published before his tenure review rolls around.)

Think through the problem you intend to address, then ask yourself: Do we know who we want to serve and why? Is serving this need consistent with our mission? Do we have the expertise to do it? Can we get our arms around this problem enough to affect it? Are we describing a need that exists in our community, or are we really describing our institution's need to put a program in place? (If your answer is the latter, go back to the top and start over.)

Question 2: What do you intend to do about the problem?

The things you plan to do about it constitute your objectives. Now, we're not talking about how you intend to remedy the problem; those ideas are your methods. Here you want to identify what will be different when you are finished implementing this program.

Is your problem that too many children in your community can't read? One of your objectives might be that, after three years, the percentage of third-graders reading at grade level will grow from 75 percent to 80 percent. About each objective you identify, ask whether you'll know when you've succeeded. If you can answer yes, that's a clear objective.

Question 3: How will you accomplish those objectives?

You've probably thought of one or more methods to achieve each objective you identified. Be very specific and very thorough. Define the activities you will engage in, step by step. Identify groups and people that will be involved. Define their roles, and dispatch someone to solicit their commitment of time and expertise.

Make a timeline: "In February, we will create public service announcements, orient the faculty who will train tutors, identify our first 50 primary-school tutors," and so on. Think through the details so that when you describe the project, your listener or reader can visualize your program and have a pretty good idea how you will spend your time and why. Methods constitute the real meat of your program. You will spend the bulk of your grant dollars on these activities. (As a reward for good planning, if you think through your methods thoroughly at this point, it will be easier to design your proposal's budget!)

When you've thought through your methods, ask yourself: If we do these things, does it make sense that we will get these outcomes? Have we omitted a step anywhere? Can I visualize how this project will accomplish our objectives? Would a reasonable person believe that with available staff and resources we can really complete these activities in the proposed timeframe? Be sure you can answer an enthusiastic yes to each question before you proceed.

Question 4: How will you know if you succeed?

The answers to this question comprise your evaluation plan, part of program planning that gets too little attention. How will you determine whether you've implemented your methods effectively and whether they actually met your objectives? In the proposal stage, your evaluation plan tells the foundation that you intend to be held accountable. At the end of the grant period, the evaluation itself will tell your funder just how successful you have been, which is likely to have a direct effect on whether it will fund your college again. The design of your evaluation plan has an effect on your ability to use the project as a demonstration project—one that shows the efficacy of certain methods for addressing an important problem and can be replicated elsewhere. It also allows your institution some measure of control over the evaluation process. If you don't do it, somebody else will—and that "somebody else" (the foundation funder, a sister institution, a journalist) might not understand your project as well as you do.

So think about what you will measure. Will you ask what you did (evaluating your success at carrying out your planned methods), whether what you did accomplished your objectives, or both? How will you measure it? Who will measure it? How will you select evaluators? Can you identify them now? How will he/she/they gather the data? With what instruments or scales? How many people will it take? What will it cost? Will it be done internally, by one of your own, or externally, by a professional evaluator or a committee of academic peers? (Give serious thought to hiring outside evaluators. That shows right up front that you're willing to have your work judged objectively—and an evaluation not biased by its managers' hopes and intentions often carries more weight.) What are the pitfalls to avoid? Will there be a final evaluation report that can be shared with the foundation? Will the results be used to fine-tune the project during its next phase? Will the results be used o expand it effectively? Answer all these questions as you and your faculty think through evaluation of your program.

Question 5: Will you sustain the program beyond the initial grant period? If so, how?

This is a key question for most foundations. After all, they don't have enough money to keep your project going forever. If you are defining and developing a service you intend to continue, you will need to think through available sources of funding to sustain the program. If you plan to work through the rough spots and then expand the program to other communities, you'll need a good sense of who might fund that expansion.

If you and your faculty group think through these questions from the start, you'll be ready to look for prospects and describe your idea to them thoroughly. And when you find a foundation that asks for a full proposal, the toughest part of writing it will be behind you.

Raising Foundation Dollars for Community Programs

YOU WILL FIND A LOT OF GOOD INFORMATION IN THIS BOOK about identifying prospects and turning them into donors. I won't repeat those ideas here except to emphasize one thing: At all costs, avoid falling into the trap of sending a proposal as a first step. Too many folks still believe that the way to raise foundation dollars is to write a terrific proposal and send it out to lots of foundations. Please don't waste your time. Raising foundation dollars is like individual fund raising in that it's the relationship that counts. Before writing a proposal, you need to know your prospect, have (or create) a link with the organization, know its current interests, and, in the great majority of cases, have a personal contact and conversation about your idea. Think of it this way: You have the best chance of having your project funded if you do your advance work so that, when your proposal arrives, a person of authority thinks to himself or herself, "Ah, yes. Here it is, just as we discussed. And I see they acted on my suggestions." Keep in mind that people give to people, and your efforts will be much more effective and far-reaching.

Now let's look at who might fund your initial community project.

Community Foundations

If your community has one, it's a natural. The community foundation exists to receive contributions from people who share an interest and commitment to the community's health and vitality. Sometimes donors give their money and tell the foundation where they would like it spent; sometimes it has priorities of its own. Either way, get to know the principals to see if your objectives might coincide with some of theirs.

Private Foundations in Your Community

These foundations have priorities much broader than your community, but because their people live and work there, some funding may be earmarked for the local area. You still need to fit into their strategic priorities—that is, be working on a problem the foundations exist to address—but the boundaries may be a little more flexible if they have funds they need to spend locally. Check with program officers you know, too. Large foundations often give senior program officers the authority to make small grants to projects nearby without having to go through the usual proposal review process.

Regional Foundations

These are often larger foundations that care about issues common to all parts of your region. Quite often, they are oriented to problems within a given state. Can your project be used as a local demonstration, then expanded to cover a broader area? If so, consider statewide and regional foundations as your prospects for expansion. But make sure your own mission is statewide or regional or you risk putting time into a program that your campus leaders won't see as strategically significant.

Family Foundations

Sometimes referred to by fund raisers as "checkbook foundations," in their simplest form these amount to a charitable entity that a family maintains, into which it makes philanthropic gifts and out of which it makes grants to worthy causes. They don't usually have professional staffs (although some have grown into the largest foundations in the United States and have extensive staffs). You can often identify, cultivate, and solicit these foundations through contact with an influential family member. Look for links between them and your institution as you would with individual prospects. Do some of them sit on your boards or working committees? (If not, there's a project that is worthy of some thought and planning.) Are they friends with any of your institution's leaders? Have they taken a recent public stand on just the issue your program addresses? Family foundations are the fastest growing group of foundations today and though they take some extra time to identify and understand, they are well worth your time.

Corporate Foundations

These organizations get their money from a for-profit company, so their strategic decision making is tied to business strategies. But community improvement is nearly always among their interests. They know their employees have to live and be happy in the community, and they want to position themselves as good corporate citizens. So don't overlook them as sources, especially if you have ties to the company and thus someone to champion your cause from within.

Expanding Your Project Regionally or Nationally

IF YOUR INSTITUTION HAS A BROADER REACH than your own community, then you may have an opportunity to expand the project into a larger region. Is the problem you addressed important to other communities? Did you address this problem in a new way? Are other communities in your institution's market as eager for help with this problem as your own was? Can you involve people in those communities as effectively as you were able to in your own? If yes, you may have a project that can be expanded.

> Corporate foundations get their money from a for-profit company, so their strategic decision making is tied to business strategies.

Here's an example. Say you're a development officer for a children's hospital that provides care both in the hospital and in the community. Leaders have been struggling with how to get good treatment to kids in underserved neighborhoods. They design a new model that gets rid of barriers and involves people in the community in a new way. You do everything right as you seek local funds for this project, and you find them from a local corporate foundation. Your project is a great success, and your evaluation tells you that kids are getting better care and are healthier than before.

But your hospital draws patients from three nearby communities as well—communities where the problem exists. To expand your project, you can look for local funds from each community. That's a good thing to do, and you may need to do it eventually. But if that's all you do, you may have to accomplish your expansion one community at a time.

Instead, think about what was new and different in the way your hospital approached the problem, and sell your program to a larger foundation as an expansion and further testing of a new model. Now your successful local project becomes a demonstration project, the results of which can be turned into an expansion across all four communities.

You'll need a foundation with strategic objectives that go beyond your community geographically. Think about foundations that care about your part of the state or the whole state. Think about corporate foundations linked to companies with operations in all four communities, that draw employees from all four communities. Get introduced, visit the right person along with the right hospital leader, and you've got a chance to expand to your entire service area.

Or, here's a different way to think about it. You finished your initial project absolutely convinced that your hospital is on to something important. You've found a way to get at a pervasive problem in a new, more effective way. Rather than look for expansion funding only in your expanded geographic area, look for a large national foundation that funds large demonstration projects that can be replicated in other states. It may not be a foundation strategically oriented toward your area or even your state. But if it cares about kids in underserved neighborhoods all across the country, and you've found a model that could work for some of them, you just might get your four-community expansion funded. In that case, the foundation's motivation is tied not to helping your area but to testing your model in a larger area to see if it might be replicable in other parts of the country.

Again, don't neglect the basics: You still need to contact a person of authority in that organization and have as much personal contact with him or her as is necessary to let them really get to know your program. A phone call is good, a personal visit better, and often best of all is to have a foundation representative visit you to see firsthand what you've done and hear about your plans for expansion.

A Proactive Approach

WHAT IF YOUR INSTITUTION HAS AN INTEREST in being part of community programs, wants to export its expertise, is willing to invest development time and resources, and has asked you how it can start in a way that could lead to programs that attract foundation funding? What can you do to facilitate synergy between your campus and your community that might yield promising community programs?

There are as many answers as there are institutions and communities, but here are a few tried and true methods worth some discussion with campus leaders and investment of time and energy:

- Search constantly for meaningful partnerships with community organizations. Find some that could join you on community-oriented programs, and think about ways that the two of you might attract funding from foundations that aren't initially interested in education.
- Get key individuals on campus to search also. Talk with people who have good community networks, and get them thinking about community collaboration possibilities.
- Encourage faculty to make presentations in the community; talk with your public relations staff about establishing a speakers bureau that could recommend speakers to community organizations on important issues.
- Encourage faculty to make themselves available as advisers to foundations with new

interests. Look out for foundations that could use the expertise of your best faculty.

- Get to know foundation executives in your community—those who make community-based grants and those who don't. You need to know them just because you live and work in the same community and your conversations might spark some ideas. Make it your business to know what they're thinking and to always have strong proposals in front of them.
- Consider establishing a regular luncheon—say, quarterly—where foundation representatives can talk with your CEO and a few key community leaders about involving the campus in issues of mutual interest.
- Find other reasons to invite foundation representatives to campus. Conferences on issues relevant to the community and of interest to your institution and local foundations are always good.
- Encourage faculty to invite community leaders into the classroom when their expertise is relevant.
- When you have a great community program, talk it up. Present it to civic groups, and have involved faculty do the same. Encourage the public relations staff to focus some attention on it. If your program falls short of expectations, talk about that, too. But be sure to explain what your institution has learned from it and leave the message that you're undaunted and intend to do more.
- Identify the regional and national foundations interested in matters important to your community and your institution. Find out what interests them most, and see if you can put together a team of institutional and community leaders to talk about it in an open-ended way. Great ideas and programs can come from these conversations.

Finally, have fun! It's real work, but few things in fund raising are as rewarding as identifying a terrific germ of an idea and finding funding for it, step by step, as it grows into a program that really has an impact on your institution and on the lives of people in your community and beyond.

Participating in a Funding Consortium

Elizabeth Loudon
Senior Associate
Copley Harris Company, Inc.

15

The 1999 *Higher Education Directory* lists more than 100 consortia, some with more than 40 members. Most are administered by independent 501(c)(3) organizations with their own large budgets. Their boards typically consist of the presidents or directors of the member institutions, with perhaps a roster of board committees and a good many standing committees. The chances are high, therefore, that if you're reading this chapter, you are already raising grant funds within an organized consortium that will approach foundations as a single institution.

If only it were so easy! As consortial leaders are wont to say, cooperation is an unnatural act. The hapless consortium administrator must seek funding for a family of institutions that tend—just like members of real families—to compete for attention, criticize one another's friends, and argue over inheritance. Consortia have no mission of their own beyond serving the institutions, even when they are themselves recipients of grant funding. The development officer or consortium director charged with writing the proposal must therefore act as diplomat, strategist, counselor, and mediator.

On the other hand, making the request as a single institution can be one of the most rewarding ventures an administrator ever undertakes. Consortial projects tend to bring unlikely people together, and the results can be far-reaching. Some foundations look for evidence of collaboration—and they're not fooled by a list of "collaborating organizations" tacked onto the end of a proposal. They want to see shared equipment and positions, collaborative training and staff and faculty development, and budgets that show, at least sometimes, reduced long-term costs for individual institutions. Some want to get the most bang for their buck; others have a more nuanced appreciation of why institutions can and sometimes should collaborate. But across the board, the chances of success are often higher if you wholeheartedly go in together.

Making that application "wholehearted" is the catch. It's a truth universally acknowledged that a single nonprofit is always in search of a partner—but the partners it has in mind are funding partners with healthy dowries, not other suitors. Nonetheless, consortial proposals can and do work well as long as all parties remember that there are several stages of collaboration. To keep the marital analogy going, I've divided the stages into three: dating, engagement, and an often polygamous marriage—with the specter of divorce never entirely absent.

The Dating Game

DATING (TO THE BEST OF MY RECOLLECTION) MEANS EVERYTHING that happens before all parties decide to form a contract. In consortial fund raising, it's all the meetings and planning and coordination that lead up to a full-fledged proposal complete with budget and a reasonable chance of success.

As in real-life dating, you will need to do the following:

1. *Find suitable prospects.* That usually means a project that's grown out of prior, voluntary collaboration—not a group of people coming together for the first time with mercenary ambitions or a group that's been created by meddlesome administrators. The most promising groups have often quietly achieved a great deal with minimal support and are thrilled to learn that they could win a grant. Sometimes a project is inspired by an ambitious visionary who can raise funds with little outside help. Encourage these take-charge types: Offer to proof and package proposals, and enjoy their success. Beware, however, of the rogue faculty member who sees a consortial enterprise as a way to bypass some pesky dean. As charming as he or she may be, you cannot be party to plans that undermine a dean's authority to call the long-term shots. Make sure, too, that your neighborhood entrepreneur isn't flirting with foundations the development office has earmarked for bigger things.

> Establish yourself as a generous colleague before you need to ask others to commit to a consortial proposal.

2. *Build trust.* Nothing enhances trust more than eating together. If you don't already meet with your consortium counterparts, start doing so now—over lunch. Play the host. If you don't have enough in your budget for meetings, fight for more. Your consortium's investment will be repaid. If you're not in a consortium but are looking for collaborators, the same rules apply.

3. *Establish yourself as a generous colleague* before *you need to ask others to commit to a consortial proposal.* Pass along all good leads. Attend professional meetings that fellow development officers helped organize. Congratulate them on grants won, especially when that same foundation just turned you down.

4. *Communicate like crazy.* Good communication is, of course, the *sine qua non* when

developing projects for funding and ensuring they're not at cross purposes with institutional priorities. As soon as collaboration is a goal, everybody needs to meet, from the board down, again and again. You probably face difficulties relating to distance, transportation, and schedules every day, but you must soldier on, knowing that a good deal of your time will be spent on logistical matters.

5. *Don't cheat.* If a member institution resists your approach to a particular foundation, no matter how irrational that resistance might seem to you, pay attention. Consortial trust matters more than a single chance at a single grant. Certainly there are cases where an institution's president has endorsed a consortial proposal despite resistance from the campus development office, and you will need to proceed, hoping that your good behavior has won you enough political capital to survive the temporary bruised feelings. But in general, trust is too precious to squander. As you develop a list of potential funding sources, therefore, check and triple-check with each member institution. When you face proprietary resistance regarding a particular foundation, consider trying the following:

A. Suggest that the resistant institution's development officer, rather than you, raise the possibility of a consortial proposal with the foundation. A surprising number will do so, especially if you've built good working relationships. The report back may be a tad skewed, but the opportunity to have the first conversation can be sufficiently reassuring to melt resistance.

B. Suggest that the consortium go in at the next funding cycle, if you can delay. If you all agree to an application time, put it in writing.

C. Suggest that you and the institution's development officer meet with the foundation officer when he or she next visits the institution. You could join them at the end of the day or for lunch—leaving the lion's share of the appointment for the institution, thus reinforcing your role as collaborator rather than competitor.

6. *Be patient.* It may take at least a year for a group of deans, department chairs, or otherwise closely linked faculty or administrators to agree on what they need funding for—let alone on what the proposal might request. Sometimes the conclusion of months of meetings will be that a group isn't ready to collaborate, at least not at a level that would attract funding. They were ready to date, but that was it.

At this stage, don't worry if you sometimes feel that consortial fund raising is like herding cats. It is like herding cats.

Rules of Engagement

ONCE YOU'RE COMMITTED TO DEVELOPING CONSORTIAL PROPOSALS, you will find that doing so can open a Pandora's box of political devils. Inevitably, one institution will feel it's carrying the burden of preparing the proposal, getting shortchanged in the budget, or both. The political feuds may seem irrational, just as squalls with new in-laws can. To stay sane and to ensure a compelling proposal, you will want to do the following:

1. *Befriend any and all financial officers in the consortium or the participating institutions,* and keep them involved with your foundation proposal planning from start to finish. Here's why:

A. There are many more fiscal variables in consortial fund raising to hammer out. For example, if a funded position resides at one of the institutions, who is responsible for receiving, investing, and reporting on the funds—the institution's financial officer or the consortium's? In the case of a long-term project, who actually approves expenditures? As often as not, it might be you. Foundations won't ask these questions—but failure to address them can result in embarrassing confusions when it comes time to report on grant expenditures.

B. Consortia typically thrive on a complex mixture of grants, contracts, and assessed fees, and these are often best understood by the financial officer. When it comes to developing a budget, you'll have to explain clearly the arrangements in place to determine such matters as assessed fees, overhead, and capital financing. You may also need to help set rates for such line items as faculty stipends, which can differ markedly among member institutions.

C. Some contractual projects managed by the financial officer may fall well outside the more familiar circle of curricular and faculty research projects. For example, the Virginia Tidewater Consortium for Higher Education had funding from the U.S. Department of Education for its Drug Use and Alcohol Abuse Prevention Program. The member colleges have subsequently assumed the costs for the program, now in its 11th year. Another consortium has federal funding for contracts with the public schools, which in turn outsource services such as career counseling and financial planning for college-bound seniors back to the consortium. You will want to be aware of such projects. They can represent an impressive vote of public confidence and may be ripe for grants.

D. Financial officers within a consortium may have excellent ideas for foundation proposals. At the Five College Consortium, a grant from the Andrew W. Mellon Foundation was conceived and administered by the five institutions' financial officers. The grant funded administrative collaboration, including risk management, recycling, student loan services, and career counseling. The impetus behind the grant was a wish to contain rising costs, and in some areas (most notably risk management) costs were indeed reduced. Other areas that don't necessarily fall directly within the financial officer's purview, such as libraries, may also follow the financial officers' lead in administrative collaboration.

E. A financial officer can be refreshingly unconcerned with campus fiefdoms and rivalries, and this neutrality will help you maintain your own steady focus on the goal.

2. *Expect dissent—you will seldom, if ever, achieve consensus.* Approaching a foundation as a single institution doesn't mean that you all agreed on everything back home. If one campus

doesn't want to get involved in a project, leave it out this time around—just be prepared to let the foundation know why, should anyone ask. Sometimes it's a simple matter of geography. In any event, genuine collaboration, as veterans of successful marriages can attest, might mean genuine sharing and compromise, but it never means sacrificing one's autonomy.

3. *Focus on shared needs and be selective, emphasizing those projects that the institutions cannot do as effectively themselves.* Projects deriving from networked technologies (as opposed to computer-based technologies, such as CD-ROM development), be they online library catalogs, distance-learning projects, or Web-site development among admissions offices, all lend themselves well to collaborative fund raising. The Alliance for Higher Education in Dallas, Texas, provides a good example. Formed in the 1960s by the co-founders of Texas Instruments, the alliance links 47 campuses, two public library systems, two school districts, and more than 30 corporations and hospitals and has won substantial grant funds for network-related technology.

At the less technical end of the spectrum, don't underestimate the political legwork necessary to create joint curricular and faculty development projects. As worthwhile as such projects can be, deans might hesitate to encourage unrealistic expectations among faculty members for longer-term support or to apply for grants that carry even the faintest threat of diminished departments. Again, the fruit of all those consortial meetings with deans and department chairs will be more wholehearted support for bold new ideas.

Don't underestimate the political legwork necessary to create joint curricular and faculty development projects.

4. *Keep your eye on the prize of creating the best programs for the institutions—not the most money for the consortium.* In all sectors, the most successful fund raisers are those who will gladly raise money even when their own departmental revenue won't grow by a cent. This last point applies especially if you work for a single institution but have been asked (or forced) to help develop a consortial proposal. You may wonder how a grant helps you if it isn't credited to your institution or if only a small portion is. First, remember that those good relationships with CFOs and other development officers will pay off: You don't need to write the whole proposal, or even attend every meeting, if you're requesting funds for a venture that breaks down into related projects at different institutions. Your friends at the collaborating institutions will help you. Next, bear in mind that foundations and senior administrators will appreciate your collegiality and your ability to help make exciting things happen, regardless of who gets the credit.

5. *Ask presidents and deans of the participating institutions to call foundations* as well as write whenever possible. Letters can be drafted for busy and important people to sign. Phone calls let the foundations know that your leaders take collaboration seriously.

Marriage . . . and Divorce

PRENUPTIAL AGREEMENTS MAY OR MAY NOT BE A GOOD THING, but their very existence points to the inevitability of conflict and change. Once a consortial arrangement is in full swing, you, as the person preparing a proposal for a foundation, need to remember the following:

1. *The grant will end—but will the relationships?* Some consortia address longer-term

funding issues up front, with written agreements about which campus will house the program if it is successful and at what cost. Others assume that a worthwhile program will find its own home in due course or will serve a short-term need but be deemed unworthy of long-term commitments. Projects with significant equipment needs can require long-term sustenance from the consortium, and that too should be discussed up front.

Foundations may press hard on this point. They don't want to contemplate an eventual divorce if they're footing the wedding bill. You can protect your institutions with wording that broadly outlines the success you will look for before incorporating a program into any institution's budget. Don't be afraid of failure. Foundation funding is usually designed to underwrite cutting-edge ventures, and even in the best consortia, some new grant-funded programs won't live up to their early promise.

2. *Don't sweat the details.* There are probably as many financing arrangements underwriting consortia as there are consortia, but the simpler the formula, the better. Each time you develop a new proposal for funding, you provoke resistance all over again, and nothing can effectively stall proposal development faster than nickel-and-dime issues of fairness. Even if one institution has to print the fliers or provide the conference site this year, the long-term goal should remain the best programs possible, not the absolute fairest arrangements.

3. *When your conciliatory efforts go unheard, have one recent and spectacular success ever at the ready.* It doesn't have to be a large grant, but it should be one that everyone agrees benefited the institutions and they couldn't have received themselves. Don't flinch at reminding people of this success and holding out the lure of more such success for their own departments and programs. (If you're new to consortial fund raising, be especially calculating about what you'll apply for. Make a request only when you're pretty sure you'll get the grant.)

4. *Don't marry* just *for the money, no matter what the foundations are telling you.* Good consortial programs are distinguished not by whether they control or reduce costs but by whether the project couldn't have been achieved by a single institution. Included in this definition would be many faculty research projects, which create what one consortium director termed "a critical mass of intellectual capital." They can be among the most exciting, for students as well as faculty. They can also be quite expensive. Be clear with funders about what will cut or contain costs and what is simply a very good idea that needs some help.

So Why Bother?

ISN'T IT EASIER TO BE SINGLE? To go to bed when you want, eat what you want—and not share your money when you make it? Although many consortial administrators find that progress is slow or that some programs atrophy after a period of funding, the benefits are myriad, and some are even self-serving. I hope I've touched on them all, but here's a quick recap:

- You can help people do things as a team that they could never do alone.

- Foundations look for evidence of collaboration.
- You might save the institutions money.
- You will develop fund-raising skills that will stand you in good stead anywhere.
- Last but not least, you will develop a broader, richer educational environment that will consequently be more competitive in the quest for faculty and students as well as grant funds—and that will enrich your life and your community as well as your consortium.

ADDITIONAL RESOURCES

Few sources exist specifically relating to consortial fund raising. Consortial administrators will surely want to read Dotolo, Lawrence G. and Jean A. Strandness, eds. *Best Practices in Higher Education Consortia: How Institutions Can Work Together.* San Francisco: Jossey-Bass, 1999.

Career Development for the Corporate and Foundation Fund-Raising Professional

Mary Kay Murphy
Vice President for Institutional Advancement
Morris Brown College
Adjunct Professor for Leadership and Organizations
Peabody College at Vanderbilt University

16

Corporate and foundation fund raising provides a wide range of opportunities for career development and growth. In the 21st century, success will come from a combination of traditional, time-honored characteristics and emerging new millennium requisites. This chapter outlines the skills and credentials of leaders in this field and suggests ways for you to develop those, too; it will also describe experience that will help your development in this profession.

Characteristics and Skills for Success

As in any profession, the most successful corporate and foundation officers have often been apprentices to other highly successful professionals, mentors who can introduce them to the requisite skills and strengths. These skills also can be acquired from individual research and study, whether it is keeping up with business and educational news services, completing a continuing education course, or attending conferences held by professional organizations. Here are a few of the most important characteristics of successful corporate and foundation officers:

Knowledge of the Institution

First and foremost, leaders in corporate and foundation fund raising embody the values and perspectives of their institutions. You must learn the history, mission, and vision of your institution and keep up with the academic interests of the faculty. To be successful, you will have to closely link your funding plans to internal priorities as set by the president, key volunteers, and faculty members. Your knowledge of higher education generally—its history, curriculum, funding, governance, ethical, legal, and political realities—and of your own institution will help you to determine whether a project or program is fundable.

First and foremost, leaders in corporate and foundation fund raising embody the values and perspectives of their institutions.

Knowing your institution will help you develop your strategic planning skills. When developing a corporate and foundation program, you must carefully consider current and future institutional funding priorities so that both the donor's and the institution's priorities are met. Take part in strategic planning committees at your institution. Understanding your institution's unique priorities will enhance your program development skills, and will help you set goals, objectives, tasks, evaluative measures, and budgets.

Strong Ethics

A strong grounding in ethics enables a successful CFR officer to earn the trust of institutional leaders and foundation and corporate personnel. While ethical development is a lifelong process, there are a number of exercises you can perform individually, or with your staff, to explore ethics. See Chapter 1 for more ideas.

Communication and Interpersonal Skills

Strengths in written and oral communication can make a corporate and foundation relations professional an expert collaborator and broker in key areas of job performance: proposal development, prospect cultivation, and program stewardship. Strong interpersonal skills are key in establishing a long-lasting network of contacts. In particular, the ability to listen and to gain consensus from a variety of institutional perspectives will help you earn trust in all of your professional interactions.

Motivation and Desire to Learn

Those who succeed in this field are internally motivated self-starters. They initiate contact, plan, organize, and evaluate. They also demonstrate a desire to continue to learn and to expand their knowledge, skills, breadth of ideas, and network of contacts.

Keeping up with the latest technology, for example, will help you develop, produce, and disseminate proposals for funding requests. The Internet will help you identify and examine corporate and foundation funding opportunities, and mastery of the Internet will let you share knowledge, information, techniques, and developments with colleagues around the world.

You'll also need to know marketing and branding opportunities to develop fundable programs. You will be expected to identify segments of marketing components to advance the strength of programs and proposals you submit.

Keep up with legislation related to tax-exempt organizations, valuing gifts of property, in-kind gifts, and gifts of outright cash and deferred gifts.

Through personal, professional, and electronic contact, develop your peer network in local, regional, national, or international grant-seeking organizations. Access to knowledge, expertise, and information gleaned from these networks helps you in setting strategic priorities, developing programs, researching projects, preparing proposals, and requesting funds.

Along with developing skills on campus, it is important to remember the importance of spending time away from campus developing long-term relationships with corporate and foundation decision makers, establishing your credentials, and building your experience.

Building Experience

Being part of successful grant applications and awards is the best way to build your experience and establish your credentials in the field of corporate and foundation fund raising. And, of course, your institution's credentials improve when it submits a well planned and well prepared proposal, is awarded the grant, and follows through with the proper use and stewardship of the gift.

One of the first steps towards participating in a successful grant application process is to develop expertise in scheduling and making effective corporate and foundation calls. You must identify the appropriate number, members, and purpose for the initial call, and must schedule it appropriately. Ideally, no more than two campus leaders call on one corporate or foundation representative—for example, the president and board chair with the funding source's president or chief executive officer. When only the president can attend a scheduled meeting with a company or foundation, the provost, a distinguished faculty member, or the vice president for institutional advancement should attend as well. Protocol also says to make one request at a time of individual funding sources—unless you disclose a simultaneous solicitation to achieve full funding of the project. Always fully disclose circumstances related to the funding request; for example, if there is the possibility that a challenge grant will be made, disclose whether you have enough prospects to complete it successfully.

In preparing to submit a request for funding, you must establish prior contact with the corporate or foundation source; demonstrate institutional financial stability and effective leadership; and show demand for the institution's services. You must present to a possible funding source a well-defined project, a compelling fund-raising strategy, and accreditation reports. Your proposal should be in an effective format and its submission should be carefully timed. In submitting a proposal, be diligent not to make common mistakes; read and adhere to funding guidelines. Do not submit the same proposal to several funding sources at one time; submit a proposal only when you have gauged the funding source's interest in the project; and disclose any problems with the program if they might affect the proposal.

In building long-term relationships with funding sources, it is essential to prove your accountability and to carry out consistent and appropriate stewardship—for example, respond promptly and thoroughly to the grant notification conditions, and keep the grant anonymous if asked. Other dimensions of successful long-term relationships include setting up the project effectively; reporting, communicating, and negotiating; and contributing timely and continuous narrative reports of results of the grant and use of the funds. Without appropriate gift reporting and stewardship, the institution holds little prospect of receiving a subsequent award from the corporate or foundation donor.

Career Paths for the Corporate and Foundation Officer

FROM TIME TO TIME, YOU'LL WANT TO DETERMINE YOUR NEXT CAREER STEP, what opportunities are available, and what new fit might be right for you. Among the first questions to ask yourself is whether to stay in the same institution, whether to move to another institution, or whether to go outside of the education setting. The characteristics, skills, credentials, and experience you gain as a corporate and foundation relations officer have many applications in the college or university setting, in other nonprofits, or outside the academy.

Skills in program development, prospect research, and proposal writing apply directly to other institutional positions, including sponsored research, campus master planning, and Title III programs. An obvious option is moving to another fund-raising operation on campus, like annual giving, major gifts, and planned giving. Success here lays the groundwork for the obvious promotion: vice president for institutional advancement.

One option is moving to the grant-making side of the funding equation, where many of the same skills are useful. Your perspective will change, however, from being the initiator and collaborator as the grant seeker to being the initiator, evaluator, and collaborator as the grant maker.

Perhaps you'll want to move to a start-up nonprofit. An enterprising and entrepreneurial corporate and foundation officer already knows how to innovate, work with limited staff and resources, market an idea, develop a board, secure seed money, expand the organization's mission and vision, and gain community leaders' confidence while growing the organization. Becoming a change agent is an exciting prospect for the confident, seasoned corporate and foundation officer.

One final career path is moving outside the academy to do market research, market analysis, or community relations. Knowledge of philanthropy and its history has far-reaching applications—from the college and university to nonprofits to grant-making community organizations.

Professional Growth and Evaluation

SUCCESS IN CORPORATE AND FOUNDATION FUND RAISING requires you to commit to steady professional growth and self-evaluation. You will be rewarded for being a self-starting collaborator and innovator, as you become known for submitting successfully funded proposals that are appropriate for the funding source and the institution.

Another dimension of professional growth and evaluation will be your contributions to institutional planning, including master planning, academic priority planning, and institutional advancement goal setting and planning. You will interact at high levels with other members of the campus development team. As you grow in the profession, you'll be invited to make presentations at professional conferences, write articles and research topics for professional publications, and conduct workshops on prospect research, proposal writing, and program development.

Corporate and foundation officers will have the opportunity this century to forge new territory in grant seeking and to build on traditional values of a nation dedicated to providing comprehensive access to higher education.

REFERENCES AND ADDITIONAL RESOURCES

American College Public Relations Association. *Greenbriar I: The Advancement of Understanding and Support of Higher Education.* ACPRA, 1958.

Council for Advancement and Support of Education. *Greenbriar II.* Washington, DC: CASE, 1988.

Drucker P. *Management Challenges for the 21st Century.* New York: Harper Business, 1999.

Heemann, P. Warren. *Criteria for Evaluating Advancement Programs.* Washington, DC: CASE, 1989.

Murphy, Mary Kay, ed. *The Advancement President and the Academy: Profiles in Institutional Leadership.* Washington, DC: American Council on Education/Oryx Press, 1997.

Murphy, Mary Kay, ed. *Building Bridges: Fund Raising for Deans, Faculty, and Development Officers.* Washington, DC: CASE, 1992.

Panas, Jerold. *Mega Gifts: Who Gives Them, Who Gets Them.* Chicago: Pluribus Press, 1986.

Panas, Jerold. *Born to Raise: What Makes a Great Fund Raiser; What Makes a Fundraiser Great.* Chicago: Pluribus Press, 1988.

Additional Resources

See also the additional resources listed at the end of several chapters.

Related CURRENTS Articles

(listed by title, author, and date)

Corporate Support

"Alderson-Broaddus Comes to Town." Dennis F. Vest, November 1975, p. 11.

"The Birth of the Blitz." Richard F. Charles, March 1976, p. 7.

"Building a Bridge from College to Business." Francis P. Hurley, March 1976, p. 9.

"Business Sense: An expert on corporate giving looks at the underpinnings of today's corporate-campus relationships." Hayden W. Smith, March 1988, p. 6.

"The Changing Face of Corporate Giving: Although businesses are looking harder at the effects of their gifts, you can still make the case for both unrestricted and restricted support." Ronald J. Kraus, February 1998, p. 10.

"Choose Your Partnership: A sampling of campus-corporate pairings." Melinda J. Burdette, March 1988, p. 18.

"The Corporate Connection: Effective company research is just like people research-on a larger scale." Carolyn E. Kourofsky, May 1992, p. 47.

"Corporate Development: Market and method." Charles W. Miersch, December 1977, p. 14.

"Corporate Fact and Fiction: How we tested four common tenets of corporate fund raising." Donald T. Cahill and Albert L. Page, May/June 1982, p. 42.

"Corporate Giving to Two-year Colleges: A study shows how companies give-and why." Richard J. Pokrass, January 1988, p. 38.

"Corporate Support: More money and involvement." Dubois S. Morris Jr., October 1979, p. 37.

"Corporations: Love 'em or leave 'em alone." Harry Warner, November 1981, p. 56.

"Courting Corporations: Instead of wine, roses, soft lights, try these 10 proven techniques." D. Chris Withers, November 1981, p. 28.

"Eye to the Future: Why corporate support is likely to increase." Frank Koch, February 1982, p. 34.

"Foreign Policy: How one university solicits corporate support internationally." John B. Shorrock, February 1988, p. 32.

"Fund Raising on Main Street." Lynda Lysakowski and Judith Snyder, January 2000, p. 34

"A Funny Thing Happened on the Way to the Harpur Forum." Fred Tamalonis, September 1979, p. 20.

"Getting in Gear: How to organize for maximum support." John Grenzebach, November 1981, p. 22.

"Getting the Business: Sometimes a change in perspective is your best route to corporate grants." Rene D. Zentner, July/August 1990, p. 40.

"Gifts that Can't Be Matched: Following recent abuse, corporations and campuses are striving to avoid further problems." William Rainbolt, January 1987, p. 12.

"Give & Take: Create a mutually beneficial relationship to bring corporate support to your campus." Rachel H. Pollack, February 1998, p. 16.

"Go Ye Into All the World: Doane College used church connections to bring its message to corporations." Terry Nygren, November/December 1985, p. 20.

"Having Double Trouble? If your matching gifts are down, use these ideas to find potential matches, spread the work, and get the gifts." Kathy Leftwich, February 1998, p. 24.

"Hispanics: Entrevista/Interview: Q: How to raise money for your Hispanic students? A: Involve your alumni and their corporate contacts." Karla Taylor, April 1983, p. 18.

"It's All in the Community: Community colleges can win corporate support." William J. Ballard, November 1981, p. 42.

"Join Hands with Lost Friends." Jeanne Knoerle, May 1978, p. 24.

"Keeping in Touch: What to do after you receive a corporate gift." Barbara LaVilla Laughton, November 1981, p. 48.

"Knowing the Field: For grant seekers, distinctions between corporate and independent foundations are lessening but still important." Lindy Keane Carter, July/August 1990, p. 34.

"Match Those Gifts!" Kerry P. McClanahan, November 1976, p. 24.

"Matching Gifts: Double, double-neither toil nor trouble." Margaret A. Bergan, November 1981, p. 44.

"Matchmaker, Matchmaker: Twenty-three ideas for encouraging corporate matching gifts from your annual fund donors." Joyce D. Koelzer, February 1992, p. 6.

"Mindpower Marches On: A sampler of corporate-campus links." Patricia LaSalle Alberger, October 1982, p. 20.

"Near and Dear: A corporate fund-raising program for small colleges." Scott Muirhead, November 1981, p. 36.

"New Approaches to the Well: Mergers. Downsizings. Losses. The news is bad for many corporations-but not necessarily for campus fund raisers." Ellen Ryan, February 1994, p. 40.

"Personalize Your Proposal Writing." Henry T. Gayley, February 1979, p. 16.

"Prof Potential Pays." Paul Solyn, May 1981, p. 33.

"Psst! Want a Match? Be wary of questionable matching gift practices." Kathy Leftwich, February 1998, p. 64.

"Spin Control: Move your grant request to the top of the pile by learning grantmakers' preferences and pet peeves." Jane C. Geever, July/August 1997, p. 38.

"Supply-Side Support: Will corporations take up the slack left by Reaganomics?" Hayden W. Smith, November 1981, p. 18.

"Time for a Thaw: British campuses and corporations had better warm up to one another." Edward G. Coll Jr., June 1987, p. 80.

"To Give or Not to Give: A day in the life of a corporate contributions officer." B.J. Nolan, November 1981, p. 14.

"Understanding the Philanthropic Partnership: Corporations don't give just to support a university; they give so the university can further philanthropic goals." Anne S. Alexander, March 1988, p. 12.

"Vesting the Interest: Corporate involvement leads to financial commitment." Peter Cummings, November 1981, p. 32.

"We Have a Lot in Common: When you convince constituents their future is linked to yours, you get partners who produce." Donald B. Edwards, February 1987, p. 60.

"What the Computer Taught Me About Corporate Alumni Gifts." Stephen G. Luther, November 1978, p. 39.

"Women Mean Business: How a women's college won corporate support." Patricia Purcell, November 1981, p. 40.

Foundation Support

"Approaching the Foundation: How to plan, prepare, and present proposals." Edwin Dieckmann, October 1977, p. 20.

"Attracting Transfers." Thomas B. Courtice, November 1978, p. 40.

"Breaking into the Foundation Big Time: A strategy for seeking grants from major foundations." Margarete R. Hall, July/August 1984, p. 18.

"Command Performance: How to garner great reviews of your visit to-or from-a foundation." Mary Margaret Walker, February 1995, p. 36.

"Foundation Gifts-Should You Seek Them?" Robert J. Finney Jr., October 1975, p. 17.

"Foundations: A new approach." William J. Farrell, September 1975, p. 20.

"The Foundations of Research: Directories, newsletters, and the Internet are the arrows in your prospect research quiver. Use them well to hit the bull's eye." Daniel Turse Jr. and Jo Anna Norris, February 1995, p. 30.

"The Foundation Stakes: It's no horse race." H. Judith Jarrell, May 1980, p. 26.

"Getting the Business: Sometimes a change in perspective is your best route to corporate grants." Rene D. Zentner, July/August 1990, p. 40.

"In the Money: A foundation president's advice on foundation solicitation." John E. Corbally, July/August 1984, p. 14.

"Knowing the Field: For grant seekers, distinctions between corporate and independent foundations are lessening but still important." Lindy Keane Carter, July/August 1990, p. 34.

"The Perfect Proposal I: The View from the Foundation: A funder's tips on avoiding the rubber stamp." Sandra A. Glass, February 1995, p. 24.

"The Perfect Proposal II: The View from Campus: A campus fund raiser tells how to cultivate foundation fruits." Barbara Stowe, February 1995, p. 25.

"Personalize Your Proposal Writing." Henry T. Gayley, February 1979, p. 16.

"Pinpointing Your Top Prospects: Three steps to target your best shot at funding." Dennis A. Prescott, February 1995, p. 32.

"Prof Potential Pays." Paul Solyn, May 1981, p. 33.

"Reach Out and Touch Someone: Use your telephone for strategic communication in foundation fund raising." Mary Kay Murphy, July/August 1984, p. 29.

"Read It and Reap: Here's a bibliography of foundation research materials." Mary Kay Murphy and Bobbie J. Strand, July/August 1984, p. 30.

"Small Can Be Beautiful: Tips on how to win grants from regional, community, and family foundations." Betsy van Patten, July/August 1984, p. 24.

"So You Want Me to Read Your Proposal." Thomas E. Broce, July/August 1982, p. 62.

"Spin Control: Move your grant request to the top of the pile by learning grantmakers' preferences and pet peeves." Jane C. Geever, July/August 1997, p. 38.

"A Winning Strategy: For victory in the home stretch, spend more time cultivating foundations and less mailing proposals." Sandra A. Glass, May 1980, p. 29.

Books

Burlingame, Dwight and Dennis Young. *Corporate Philanthropy at the Crossroads.* Bloomington, IN: Indiana University Press, 1996.

CASE. *Donor Relations: The Essential Guide to Stewardship Policies, Procedures, and Protocol.* Washington, DC: CASE Books, 1999.

Gooch, Judith Mirick. *Writing Winning Proposals.* Washington, DC: CASE Books 1987.

Murphy, Mary Kay. *Advancement President and the Academy.* Washington, DC: ACE/Oryx Press, 1997.

Murphy, Mary Kay, ed. *Building Bridges: Fund Raising for Deans, Faculty and Development Officers.* Washington, DC: CASE, 1992.

Murphy, Mary Kay, ed. *Cultivating Foundation Support for Education.* Washington, DC: CASE Books, 1989.

Worth, Michael J., ed. *Educational Fund Raising: Principles and Practice.* Phoenix: ACE/Oryx Press, 1993.

Buchanan, Peter. ed. *Handbook of Institutional Advancement,* Third Edition. Washington, DC: CASE Books, 2000. (To be released in Spring 2000.)

Indexes and Periodicals

Chronicle of Higher Education, a weekly publication

Chronicle of Philanthropy, a bi-weekly publication

Council on Foundation's Foundation News and Commentary, a bi-monthly magazine.

The Foundation Center's *The Foundation Directory,* 20th edition. (1998)

The Foundation Center's *The Foundation Grants Index,* 27th edition. (1999)

The Foundation Center. *FC Search:* CD-ROM Database. (1998)

The Taft Group's *The Foundation Reporter,* 30th edition. (1998)

Online Resources

CFRnet, a listserve of corporate and foundation fund raising for educational institutions. To subscribe, send an e-mail to *listproc@medicine.wustl.edu.*

American Philanthropy Review: *http://philanthropy-review.com/forums*

Association of Governing Boards of Universities and Colleges: *www.agb.org*

Chronicle of Philanthropy: *www.philanthropy.com*

Council for Advancement and Support of Education: *www.case.org*

Council on Foundations: *www.cof.org*

The Foundation Center: *www.fdncenter.org*

Foundation Commons (Grantmakers Electronic Proposal Processing System): *www.gepps.org*

Foundation for Independent Higher Education: *www.fihe.org*

GrantsWeb: *www.web.fie.com*

National Association of College Business Officers: *www.nacubo.org*

National Association of Independent Schools: *www.nais.org*

National Society of Fund Raising Executives: *www.nsfre.org*

Philanthropy Journal Online: *www.philanthropy-journal.org*

Contributors

Mary Kay Murphy is vice president for institutional advancement at Morris Brown College in Atlanta, Georgia and adjunct professor of Leadership and Organizations at Peabody College at Vanderbilt University. She has served as editor for three previous books on fund raising for CASE and for the American Council on Education. In 1999, she received CASE's Warwick Award for Outstanding Original Research for her book *The Advancement President and the Academy: Profiles in Institutional Leadership.* In 1994, she received CASE's Alice Beeman Award for Excellence in Advancement Writing. She served on the CASE International's Board and as Chair of CASE District III. She is on the editorial board for CASE's new *International Journal of Educational Advancement*.

Alan Bloomgarden is assistant director of faculty grants and government relations at Smith College. He worked for 10 years with non-governmental organizations (NGOs) in disarmament and international affairs, and is an education activist in his hometown of Hatfield, Massachusetts.

Michael Brennan, head of UCLA's corporate, foundation, and research relations office, has 15 years of experience in the corporate and foundation relations profession.

Kevin Doody is director of corporate relations at the California Institute of Technology. He is a member of the Academic Advisory Council of the Industrial Research Institute's University Relations Committee. He received his master's degree from the University of California, Davis, and his bachelor's degree from California State University, Los Angeles.

Patricia Gregory, senior director of corporate and foundation relations at Washington University School of Medicine in St. Louis, is a regular presenter at CASE conferences and manages CFRnet, the Internet discussion group for corporate and foundation fund raising in education. She earned a Ph.D. in physiology and biophysics in 1986, and spent several years in biomedical research before undertaking training in academic leadership and moving into development work.

Cathy Hanby-Sikora is the principal consultant with Hanby-Sikora & Associates, Inc., based in Chapel Hill, North Carolina. She served Duke University as director of foundation relations and as associate dean of the Nicholas School of the Environment, and she served the Duke University Medical Center as director of corporate and foundation relations.

G.A. (Jay) Hartford retired from the University of Michigan in 1999 as senior director of corporate & foundation relations. His previous roles in higher education included 19 years as a vice president for business and finance at two universities: Washington State University and Ferris State University in Michigan.

F.A. (Ski) Hilenski has worked in the advancement profession for over twenty years, and is currently director of development for the Ivan Allen College of Liberal Arts at Georgia Institute of Technology. Hilenski received his A.B. from Pfeiffer College, and his M.A. and Ph.D. (in English) from the University of Tennessee, Knoxville. He has been honored with several academic and professional awards, and is accredited as an Advanced Certified Fund Raising Executive by the National Society of Fund Raising Executives.

Larry D. Lauer is associate vice chancellor for communications and public affairs at Texas Christian University in Fort Worth, Texas. He is director of the Commission on the Future of TCU, Chairman of the University's Marketing Advisory Board and Advisory Committee, member of the Chancellor's Cabinet, and Assistant Professor of Corporate Communications. He also teaches international communication at TCU's London Center. He is author of the book *Communication Power: Energizing Your Nonprofit Organization* and more than 20 other articles and chapters about marketing and communications.

Geoff Liggett is a Boston-based fund-raising consultant. He has worked for three major universities in their corporate, foundation and international development efforts. Most recently he served as director of corporate and foundation relations at Carnegie Mellon University.

Elizabeth Loudon raised grant funds at the Five College Consortium in Amherst for five years. She is now an independent consultant in the greater Boston area.

Patricia Martin has been director of corporate and foundation relations at Carleton College since 1988. Previously, she was a newspaper reporter, college professor, and director of the Carleton News Bureau.

Ken Spritz is a fund-raising consultant from Hanover, New Hampshire, who previously worked for nine years as Dartmouth College's director of foundation and corporate relations.

Robin Torbron-Warde has 16 years' experience in corporate and foundation relations at both large and small institutions and is currently at Brown University. She had editorial advice preparing her chapter from Sandra Zommer, assistant director of corporate and foundation relations at Wheaton College, where Ms. Warde served as director from 1993 through 1999.

Kent Weeks is a practicing attorney in Nashville, Tennessee and a professor of the Practice of Education at Peabody College at Vanderbilt University. He is the author of *Institutional Advancement and the Law* (College Legal Information, Inc., 1999.)

Bruce Wyatt, a graduate of Knox College and the University of Iowa, has held administrative positions and has taught at the School for International Training, Mount Holyoke College, and Beloit College. He is currently vice president for external affairs at Beloit College.